ROD'S SUDOKU
TUTORIAL

RODNEY L. WAGNER

Sample puzzles 1, 2, and 3 are reproduced from *Dell Original Sudoku*, November
2016, puzzles 69, 44, and 77. Used with permission of Dell Publications.

Sample puzzle 4 (used in part 3) was reproduced from *Dell Original Sudoku*, magazine dated
November 2016, puzzle number 203. Used with permission of Dell Publications.

Archway Publishing books may be ordered through booksellers or by contacting:

Archway Publishing
1663 Liberty Drive
Bloomington, IN 47403
www.archwaypublishing.com
1 (888) 242-5904

ISBN: 978-1-4808-5405-5 (sc)
ISBN: 978-1-4808-5404-8 (e)

Library of Congress Control Number: 2017917041

Print information available on the last page.

Archway Publishing rev. date: 12/11/2017

My sister-in-law, Alice, by chance saw that I worked sudoku. She asked if I could teach her my techniques.

I said yes and started an outline so I would be sure to cover most of the essentials and techniques I use to solve puzzles. Later I began adding details and compiled examples, which eventually became this tutorial.

My wife, Sharon, encouraged me during the earlier periods of writing my outline and notes. Then, when the tutorial was finished, she greatly encouraged me to publish the book.

And so I have.

Thank you, Alice and Sharon,

and to you both, I dedicate *this book*

and all my efforts!

CONTENTS

WELCOME LETTER

June 2017

Dear Alice (and all other sudoku enthusiasts):

I am thrilled you have been introduced to sudoku and desire to solve the puzzles. Sudoku is fun, challenging, and sometimes frustratingly difficult. I hope you will find this book, *Rod's Sudoku Tutorial*, helpful, whether you are a novice or have a moderate amount of experience and are seeking to improve your skills.

Ed introduced me to sudoku in the summer of 2005, and I have probably worked over 2,500 puzzles since then and continue to do so. I was told only the three basic rules of sudoku and was shown a copy of a newsstand sudoku puzzles magazine. I purchased a copy, read the introduction, and went to work at the beginning, where the easy-rated puzzles are located. I worked nearly 400 easy puzzles before I even looked at the medium puzzles. I have now successfully solved scores of hard puzzles and even some extreme puzzles.

I have often made blank grids (see Illustration 13, Appendix), filled in the givens in ink, and reworked many puzzles (in pencil) after I had worn holes in the original copy from writing and then erasing in them. (I have done this so many times I can't remember.)

Go for it. If you get stuck, don't get frustrated; set *that* puzzle aside for some time, and try a different one.

Above all, *enjoy sudoku*!

/s/ Rodney L. Wagner

INTRODUCTION

These tutorial techniques are the result of my personal experience after I was introduced to sudoku and had read the brief introductions found in the front of sudoku publications like the ones published by Dell and Kappa. There is no magic! Any technique is *primarily* simple logic applied to the basic rules of sudoku. You simply have to find the *right* digit to enter into an empty cell or eliminate the digits that can*not* be entered into an empty cell.

In this tutorial, I attempt to give instructions and show by example how to solve an *entire* puzzle, step by step, from beginning to end. I *sequentially* use *each* digit 1 through 9 in each technique. With this method, I know when I am done and am confident I have been complete and exhaustive; I have not missed any possible play. (But I always check my work and the answers anyway.) From these instructions and examples, I hope you will be able to gain enough information to go on and solve many puzzles on your own.

Before you start a sudoku puzzle, orient yourself to the puzzle. (See illustration 1.) The puzzle is a large square containing nine rows and nine columns with each containing nine small squares. The total puzzle is subdivided into nine square sections with each section consisting of three contiguous rows and three contiguous columns. These sections are usually indicated by heavier lines. All the small squares formed by the intersection of a row and a column are called cells. To identify *each* cell *uniquely*, it will be referenced (in this tutorial and elsewhere) by section, row, and column (e.g., S5R7C4). Further, each section, row, and column may be referenced individually or in combination (e.g., S3; R9; C5; S5R6, or S2R2 and 3; S7C7 and 8; and so on). Every puzzle comes with a certain number of digits with a varying number of occurrences already placed in various cells in the puzzle; these are *given* to you as a starting point, and thus they are called *givens*.

The objective is for you to find the *right* digit for each and every one of the empty cells. When the puzzle is completely solved, each row, each column, and each section will have *one* and *only* one occurrence of each digit 1 through 9. (This may seem a restatement of the three basic rules, but it is of utmost importance to keep these rules in mind as you solve the puzzle.)

Sudoku puzzles are rated in four basic classes: very easy, easy, medium, and hard (some puzzle publishers classify them differently). These ratings are simply a *general* guide to their difficulty and are based on several criteria. Beyond the hard-rated puzzles, you can find even harder puzzles called "extreme," "devilish," "challenging," and so on. As you increase in difficulty, the puzzles will have *fewer givens* and fewer occurrences of each *given* digit, and they are strategically placed to be more difficult. Most newsstand sudoku magazines contain a number of puzzles in each rating. And you can find sudoku puzzles with different variations to add to the fun; I do not discuss any variations in this tutorial.

This tutorial is divided into three parts. Part 1 is intended primarily for but not limited to the beginner, who has never attempted to work on a sudoku puzzle but is curious and has a desire to start. Part 2 helps you solve almost all the medium-rated puzzles, which I call the intermediate level. Part 3 contains advanced techniques and actions required in solving the hard-rated puzzles.

This tutorial contains *my* techniques, examples, and illustrations. However, I used actual sample puzzles in the "Working Exercises" in Part 1. I also included two additional sample puzzles so you can actually practice the techniques. There is a fourth sample puzzle as an example in part 3. Oh, yes, I have included copies of the answers.

If I have one self-criticism of this tutorial, it is that I have been *extremely restrictive*; I have tried very hard to separate the techniques and not to combine them in part 1 of this the tutorial.

That is, if you are to look for a *pair* of digits in a group, I have attempted to avoid any reference to any *single* digit. I was also very restrictive by emphasizing increasing your digit *in sequence* from 1 through 9; I never returned to a lower digit (e.g., when using the digit 7 and it opened an entry for the digit 3, I passed it *until* the next iteration). I have done this to build foundational skills. However, in the later techniques, I may bounce back to an earlier technique and solve another cell and then return to the current higher technique. This statement is not intended to detract from the ability of the human mind to multitask.

Section 1		Section 2		Section 3	
Section 4		Section 5		Section 6	
Section 7		Section 8		Section 9	

Illutration 1a showing section numbers

Row 1
Row 2
Row 3
Row 4
Row 5
Row 6
Row 7
Row 8
Row 9

Illustration 1b showing row numbers

c	c	c	c	c	c	c	c	c
o	o	o	o	o	o	o	o	o
l	l	l	l	l	l	l	l	l
u	u	u	u	u	u	u	u	u
m	m	m	m	m	m	m	m	m
n	n	n	n	n	n	n	n	n
1	2	3	4	5	6	7	8	9

Illustration 1c showing column numbers

	5		2					3
		7			1		9	
1		6			7	5		2
		4	7	5		3	2	
5					9			8
	1	3		4	2	7		
7		1	6				9	4
	2		4			8		
4				8		1		

Illustration 1d showing the three Horizontal Section Groups.

Illustration 1: The layout and names of the SUDOKU puzzle.

PART 1
The Beginnings

Horizontal Section Group Scans

Stop! Have you read the introduction and studied illustration 1 showing the puzzle's layout and labels for the different parts of the sudoku puzzle? If not, go back and do it *now*. I reference that information heavily in the tutorial to show the locations of cells being solved.

This is a tutorial. I expect you to work the puzzles I have provided as you study this book. Therefore, make a copy of the sample puzzle 1 (illustration 2) to use as we do the working exercises together.

	5		2					3
		7			1		9	
1		6			7	5		2
		4	7	5		3	2	
5				9				8
	1	3		4	2	7		
7		1	6			9		4
	2		4			8		
4					8		1	

Illustration 2: Sample puzzle 1 to Use in "Working Exercises" in Techniques 1 throug 4.

1

I have also included a copy of it after we have completed it (i.e., the answers; see the appendix). This is for you to check your own work. The working exercises are separated from the body of text by horizontal lines, the use of a second font, and indentation. The working exercises follow the narrative; study the narrative first and then work the exercises.

As you complete each working exercise in order as numbered, be aware that I have purposefully reduced the amount of explanation at several subsequent points. To be successful, I recommend you follow the full sequence of the procedure; I always do that myself.

Technique 1 starts with a scan of the first horizontal section group (i.e., S1, 2 and 3) and with the digit 1, which will be increased by 1 until it reaches 9. Then you will drop down to the second horizontal group (i.e., S4, 5, and 6) and repeat this technique with digits 1 through 9, with each repetition. Then you will drop down once more to the third (bottom) horizontal section group 3 (i.e., S7, 8, and 9). Each scan will start with digit 1 and be increased by one until it reaches digit 9.

The basic procedure for technique 1 is to scan the horizontal section group and look for *two* occurrences *(a pair)* of the same digit number as the iteration (1 through 9) in any two of the three sections and any two of the three rows. (In other words, the first time through this technique, you will be looking for *two occurrences* of the digit 1; the second time, you will look for two occurrences of the digit 2, and so on). Be sure to scan all three sections *and* all three rows in the horizontal section group for the number. Note—there will *always* be one iteration (and probably more) in this technique when you will *not* find two occurrences of the digit for which you are scanning. You might not even find a single occurrence of a specific digit. Do not worry. Simply increase your digit by 1 and repeat the scan.

When you find a digit with only two occurrences in the horizontal section group, focus on the one *section* and the one *row* that does *not* have that digit. In that section and row, at least one cell *must* be empty, and all three cells might be empty.

If there is only one empty cell, it is easy; enter the digit in that cell. Then add 1 to your digit and repeat the scan.

When there are two empty cells in the row, you will have to scan the intersecting columns for each of the empty cells for an occurrence of the digit matching the iteration number in the entire column spanning all nine rows. If *either* column does not have an occurrence of the digit and the other column does have an occurrence of the digit, it is the column without the occurrence of the digit in which you can correctly enter the digit in the empty cell at the original cell location (section, row, and column). To say this instruction another way, if the digit is found in either column that you scanned, you *cannot* use that column that contains your digit. If your digit is *not* found in either column, you cannot decide into which empty cell in the row to enter your digit at the originating location; it must be left unsolved for this iteration.

When you have completed all of the above with digit 1, add 1 to your digit and repeat this entire technique until you have examined all three horizontal section groups with *all* the digits, 1 through 9.

Do the following working exercises for this technique before going on to technique 2.

Working Exercise 1

Study the sample puzzle. Focus on the first horizontal section group, and start with the digit 1. Immediately, you see that a 1 appears in sections 1 and 2, in rows 3 and 2. That leaves cells S3R1C7 and 8 available for the digit 1. Scanning the intersecting *columns* 7 and 8 for a digit 1, you find the digit in S9R9C8, but you do not find the digit 1 in any cell in column 7. Therefore, enter a 1 in S3R1C7.

Increase your digit to 2, and you find a 2 in S2 and 3, R1 and 3, leaving S1R2C1 and 2 available for the digit 2. Scan the intersecting columns 1 and 2 for the digit 2. You do not find the digit 2 in any cell in column 1, but it is found in S7R8C2. Therefore, enter digit 2 in S1R2C1 (i.e. the column without the digit).

Increase your digit to 3, and you find only one 3 in S3R1C9. You cannot work it because you are looking for *pairs* of the digit, so increase your digit to 4. There are no 4s in this first horizontal section group, so increase your digit to 5. A 5 occurs in S1 and 3, R1 and 3, leaving S2R2C4 and 5 for the digit. Scan C4 and 5 for a 5. You do not find a 5 in C4, but you do find a 5 in S5R4C5. Enter the 5 in S2R2C4.

Increase your digit to 6. There is only one digit 6 in this horizontal section group, so increase the digit to 7. A 7 occurs in S1 and 2 and R2 and 3, so we have to look at S3R1, where only C8 is empty. (Scanning C8 finds no other 7 in the column; this is just a double check on our accuracy so far. It is a good practice to double-check your work *frequently*). Enter the 7 in S3R1C8.

Increase your digit to 8, and there is no occurrence of the digit in this section. Increase to 9 and there is only one occurrence. So we are done with the first horizontal section group.

Working Exercise 2

Exercise 2 will focus on the second, or middle, horizontal section group (i.e., sections 4, 5, and 6). The process is exactly like exercise 1.

Start with the digit 1 increasing it through 9.

Digit 1—there is only one occurrence, which cannot be used. Increase digit to 2.

Digit 2 occurs in S5 and 6, R6 and 4 (working left to right); S4R5 needs digit 2; C2 is eliminated by the 2 occurring in S7R8C2. Enter 2 in S4R5C3, and increase digit to 3.

Digit 3—there are two occurrences, but we are unable to place 3 in S5R5, as either of the two empty cells could contain a 3 as *neither* vertical column has a 3. Increase digit.

Digit 4 has the same situation as digit 3. Increase digit.

Digit 5 is the same situation as digit 4. Increase digit.

Digit 6—there is no occurrence. Increase digit.

Digit 7—S5 and 6 R4 and 6 (left to right) contain 7; this leaves S4R5 as needing a 7. One cell remains empty (S4R5C2) since we have entered a 2 in C3. (Double-check the columns, and we are okay.) Enter the 7 in S4R5C2. Increase digit.

Digit 8—there is only one occurrence, which cannot be used. Increase digit.

Digit 9 is the same situation as digit 8.

Working Exercise 3

Exercise 3 will focus on the third, or bottom, horizontal section group (i.e., sections 7, 8, and 9). The process is exactly like exercises 1 and 2.

Start with the digit 1 increasing it through 9.

Digit 1 is found in S7 and 9, R7 and 9, *and* in column S2R2C6; that leaves only one cell for you to enter 1 in, S8R8C5.

Digit 2 has only one occurrence, which cannot be used.

Digit 3—there is no occurrence.

Digit 4 occurs in all three sections and rows.

Digit 5 has no occurrence.

Digits 6 and 7—there is only one occurrence of each, which cannot be used.

Digit 8 is found in S8 and 9, R9 and 8; enter 8 in S7R7C2. (This is the only empty cell in the section and row.)

Digit 9 has only one occurrence, which cannot be used.

We have completed technique 1. Go to technique 2.

TECHNIQUE 2

Vertical Section Group Scans

The second technique is identical to the first technique, except it starts with the first *vertical* section group (i.e., sections 1, 4, and 7). Again, we start with the digit 1 and increase it by 1 (through digit 9) with each successive iteration of this technique.

The basic procedure for this technique is to scan each vertical section group and look, as you did in technique 1, for *two* occurrences *(a pair)* of the same digit number as the iteration (1 through 9) in any *two* of the three sections and any *two* of the three columns. Be sure to scan all three sections and all three columns for the number. Note—there will *always* be one iteration (and probably more) in this technique when you will *not* find two occurrences of the digit for which you are scanning. You might not even find a single occurrence of a specific digit. Do not worry. Simply increase your digit by 1, and repeat the scan.

When you find a digit with *two* occurrences, focus on the section *and* column that does *not* have the digit for which you are scanning. In the section and column, at least one cell must be empty, and possibly all three cells will be empty.

If there is only one empty cell, it is easy: enter the digit in that cell. Then increase your digit by 1 and repeat this technique.

When there are two empty cells in the column, you will have to scan the intersecting *rows* for each of the empty cells for the digit iteration in the entire row spanning all columns (1 through 9). If either row does *not* have an occurrence of the digit and the other row does *have* an occurrence of the digit, it is the row without the

7

occurrence of the digit in which you can correctly enter the digit at the original cell location (section, row, and column). To say this instruction another way, if the digit is found in either row that you scanned, you can*not* use that row; use the other row. If your digit is *not* found in either row of the other two sections, you cannot decide into which empty cell in the column to enter your digit at the originating location. Wait for a later iteration.

When you have completed this process with digit 1, increase your digit by 1 and repeat the entire technique until you have examined all three groups of vertical sections with *all* the digits 1 through 9.

The working exercises follow for you to work now.

Working Exercise 4

Using the same sample puzzle that we have started, start with the leftmost vertical section group and with the digit 1. Look for two occurrences of it.

Digit 1—three sections and columns are completed.

Digit 2—three sections and columns are completed.

Digit 3 has only one occurrence, cannot use.

Digit 4—we cannot determine which empty cell to use; digit not in crossing rows.

Digit 5 is the same situation as digit 4.

Digit 6 has only one occurrence, cannot use.

Digit 7—three sections and columns are completed.

Digit 8 has only one occurrence, cannot use.

Digit 9 has no occurrence in this section group.

Move your focus to the second or middle vertical section group, and repeat this procedure.

Digit 1 occurs in S2 and 8, C5 and 6, *and* in row S4R6C2, leaving only S5R5C4 for the 1. Enter 1 in S5R5C4.

Digit 2 has two occurrences, cannot determine which empty cell to use; digit not in intersecting rows.

Digit 3—there is no occurrence in this section group.

Digit 4—enter a 4 in S2R1C6, which is the only empty cell available in S2C6.

Digit 5—we cannot determine which empty cell to use.

Digit 6 has only one occurrence, cannot use.

Digit 7—occurs in S2 and 5, C4 and 6, *and* in row S7R7C1, leaving only S8R9C5 for the 7. Enter the 7 in S8R9C5.

Digit 8 has only one occurrence, cannot use.

Digit 9 has only one occurrence, cannot use.

Move your focus to the third, or rightmost, vertical section group, and repeat this procedure.

Digit 1—enter a 1 in S6R4C9.

Digit 2—enter a 2 in S9R9C7.

Digit 3—we cannot determine which empty cell to use.

Digit 4 has only one occurrence, cannot use.

Digit 5 has only one occurrence, cannot use.

Digit 6 has no occurrence in this section group.

Digit 7—occurs in S3 and 6, C7 and 8, *and* in rows S7R7C1 *(and also S9R7C9 already has a given)* and S8R9C5, leaving only S9R8C9 for the 7. Enter the 7 in S9R8C9.

Digit 8—enter an 8 in S3R3C8.

Digit 9—enter a 9 in S6R6C9.

We have completed technique 2; go to technique 3.

Repeating Techniques 1 and 2

Repeat techniques 1 and 2 *until* you have *not made any change* to the puzzle (i.e., you have not entered any digit into any cell *either* horizontally or vertically *in the iteration*). Repeating this technique is required *because* anytime you enter a digit into an empty cell, you *change* the quantities of the digit or have eliminated a cell or cells from your consideration. *Some* puzzles may require *up to seven* or even more repetitions of this technique. This may seem monotonous, but we must fill *all* the cells we can using these first two simple techniques before we go on to technique 4.

(I promise the repetitions will become increasingly easier and quicker with practice. Therefore, bear the monotony for now.)

Working Exercise 5

Using our sample puzzle we have worked thus far, we start technique 3. Begin repeating technique 1. Scan the top or first horizontal section group, using the digit 1, increasing it by 1 with each successive iteration through 9. Remember, you are still looking for a *pair* (two occurrences) of the same digit. (This is iteration 1 of the horizontal section groups.)

Digit 1—all three sections and rows are completed.

Digit 2 is the same as 1.

Digits 3 and 4 have only one occurrence each, cannot use.

Digit 5—all three sections and rows are completed.

Digit 6 has only one occurrence, cannot use.

Digit 7 occurs in all three sections and rows.

Digit 8 has only one occurrence, cannot use.

Digit 9 has only one occurrence, cannot use.

Move to the middle horizontal section group, and repeat the procedure.

Digit 1—all three sections and rows are completed.

Digit 2—all three sections and rows are completed.

Digit 3—enter a 3 in S5R5C6, which is the only cell available in that section and row.

Digit 4—there are two occurrences, cannot determine which cell to use.

Digit 5— enter the 5 in S6R6C8, as it is only cell available in that section and row.

Digit 6—there is no occurrence in this section group.

Digit 7—all three sections and rows are completed.

Digit 8 has only one occurrence, cannot use.

Digit 9—there are two occurrences, cannot determine which cell to use.

Move to the bottom horizontal section group, and repeat the procedure.

Digit 1—all three sections and columns are completed.

Digit 2—enter 2 in S8R7C5.

Digits 3 through 9: no actions possible.

We have completed the first iteration of scanning of all three *horizontal* section groups for this technique 3. Continue with the next working exercise, 6, where we will work the vertical section groups for this technique 3.

Working Exercise 6

Still using our sample puzzle, we will start at the first, or leftmost, vertical section group (in this first iteration of the vertical section groups) and work technique 2.

No actions are possible in this first vertical section group. (Check it out! Do the scan for all digits 1 through 9.)

Focus on the middle, or second, vertical section group.

No actions are possible in this middle vertical section group. (Check it out! Do the scan for all digits 1 through 9.)

Focus on the rightmost, or third, vertical section group.

No actions are possible in this rightmost vertical section group.

We have finished the first complete iteration of technique 3 (repeating techniques 1 and 2), which made some changes to the puzzle; therefore, we must repeat technique 3 once more, which requires us to repeat techniques 1 and 2 again.

Working Exercise 7

Beginning with the first horizontal section group, scan all three horizontal section groups. (This begins iteration 2 of technique 3.)

In horizontal section group 1, no entry is possible.

In horizontal section group 2, no entry is possible.

In horizontal section group 3, no entry is possible.

Now scan all three vertical section groups.

In vertical section group 1, no entry is possible.

In vertical section group 2, no entry is possible.

In vertical section group 3,

Digit 5—enter the 5 in S9R9C9.

We changed one cell; repeat the is technique again.

In horizontal section group 1, no entry is possible.

In horizontal section group 2, no entry is possible.

In horizontal section group 3, no entry is possible.

Now scan all three vertical section groups.

In vertical section group 1,

Digit 5—enter the 5 in S7R8C3.

In vertical section group 2,

Digit 5—enter the 5 in S8R7C6.

In vertical section group 3, no entry is possible.

Since we made entries in the last iteration, one more is needed.

No changes were made.

We have finished several iterations of technique 3 and no changes were made to our puzzle in the last iteration. But since we still have empty cells in our sample puzzle, we need to go on to technique 4 for additional actions which we can take to complete our puzzle.

TECHNIQUE 4

Working Single-Digit Occurrences

Note: The examples in this technique were created by the author for illustrative purposes only; they do not relate in any way to the sample puzzle 1 that we started (and worked) in the previous three techniques. However, for the Working Exercise 8 (in this technique) you will need to continue using the sample puzzle 1 that you have worked thus far; so keep it handy.

Since you have completed multiple iterations and repetitions of technique 3 and still have some empty cells, technique 4 (and technique 5 in part 2) will give you renewed hope and help you finish the puzzle. In techniques 1 through 3 you looked for a *pair* of digits and entered digits into cells matching your work digit (iteration). In contrast, this technique works when you have either a pair *or only one* given or entered occurrence of the digit for which you are looking.

The purpose of this technique is to *eliminate* rows, columns, or cells to find a single cell into which you can correctly enter your digit. Whether you have a single cell or multiple cells or single or multiple rows or columns available, you need to be able to *eliminate* one or more of them with this technique, possibly leaving only the *right* cell into which you can enter your digit. Yes, you have used this idea in simpler situations in earlier techniques (scanning intersecting rows and columns), but this technique looks at more difficult situations and shows you the way and reason to go forward. This is an important and helpful technique that you could use as a stand-alone technique or in combination with any other technique.

There are three situations you could have where you need this technique (single cell, multiple cells, and multiple cells spanning multiple rows or columns). I discuss these separately as situations A, B, and C.

The following paragraph is the procedure for this technique, which may need to be repeated any number of times.

You will scan each horizontal and vertical section group sequentially using each digit 1 through 9. If you have a pair and can uniquely and correctly enter the digit in a single empty cell, do so. However, if you have only a single occurrence of the digit, use the following examples to try to find the unique and correct cell for your digit. And it is possible, especially in the initial iterations, you may not be able to enter a digit. *Do not force an entry*! And *do not guess*!

Remember to work every horizontal and every vertical section group and repeat the procedure as needed. You may be surprised at how many puzzles, through medium-rated ones, can be solved completely with this technique.

Situation A: Single Cell Available in a Section

Although illustration 3 shows this situation in horizontal format, it may also occur in vertical format.

Scan the horizontal and vertical section groups, increasing your digit 1 through 9, as we have done previously, but this time, look for either a pair *or* only a single occurrence of your digit in any one of the three sections in a group. See illustration 3, which demonstrates this situation that often exist in sudoku puzzles. Do you see the digit 4 in S1R2C1. Scan the other rows in the other two horizontal (or vertical) sections, searching for a cell into which you can enter a 4.

5	6		8	3				9
4							2	
		9	2	7	1	5	3	

A. Original GIVENS in puzzle

5	6		8	3	4			9
4							2	
		9	2	7	1	5	3	

B. First digit 4 solved

5	6		8	3	4			9
4							2	
		9	2	7	1	5	3	4

C. Second digit 4 solved.

Illustration 3 Sowing solution when one cell is available.

Since the 4 already occurred in S1R2, that entire row (R2) is eliminated from any further entry of the 4. In the second section, note that the third (or bottom [R3]) row already has all three cells occupied, so they are also eliminated from any further entry into them by any digit. Since we have just eliminated R2 and 3, the first or top row in the second section (S2R1) has only one empty cell available for entry of the digit 4. Enter the 4 in cell S2R1C6. (Note that in the middle (B) portion of the illustration, I have enlarged the entry and shaded the background of the cell to highlight it.)

Pause! It is perfectly permissible (and even advantageous) to *reuse* an *earlier* technique at any point it helps to solve the puzzle. Then return to the point where you left, and continue with this technique.

At this point, do you remember the *first* technique (scan a horizontal section group for two occurrences of the digit)? We now have that situation, in illustration 3, with the digit 4 occurring in S1R2C1 and S2R1C6. So looking at the third section, we can readily see that there is only one empty cell in the bottom row, S3R3C9. Enter the digit 4 there. (Again, I have enlarged the entry in the lower portion of the illustration and shaded the background of the cell to highlight it.) In summary, *if* and when, working any puzzle you have a situation like situation A in illustration 3, first solve the cell and then reuse the tools from technique 1 (or 2) to help solve additional cells in the same group in the puzzle.

Situation B: Multiple Cells Available in the Same Row or Column

Although illustration 4 shows this situation in vertical format, it may also occur in horizontal format.

In the previous situation, there was only one empty cell in each of the two sections and rows in which to enter the digit. Thus, the decision to enter the digit was relatively easy to make. When you have two or more empty cells available for the digit, the decision becomes more complex and more difficult, but here's how to solve it.

The most important thing to do is to *decide* which cell you can *eliminate* (i.e., in which cell you cannot correctly enter your digit) and which cell you can use to correctly enter your digit. See illustration 4 and follow the narrative here.

Illustration 4: Partial puzzle showing solution with multiple cells available.

Locate the digit 5 in the top section (S1R1C3). It is the only occurrence of the digit 5 in the vertical section group (i.e., a *single* occurrence). This part of the technique will guide you through processes necessary to solve many situations where you have a single occurrence of a digit and multiple empty cells available in either the same row or the same column in the vertical (or horizontal) section group for entry of the digit.

In the top section, the 5 is in the last column (C3), and that causes the entire column 3 to be eliminated from containing another 5 in any cell in that column. Therefore, focus on the middle section. All cells in the first column are already filled and are automatically eliminated from further consideration of any entry. That leaves the two empty cells in the middle column. In which one of the cells can we correctly enter the 5?

The answer lies in the second horizontal section of the middle horizontal group. There is a 5 in the bottom row of that section, and following that row back to the first section (in the vertical section group), we eliminate the cell in the bottom row of the middle column in the vertical section group. This leaves only the top cell in the middle column of the middle section of the vertical section group into which we can enter the 5 accurately. The right portion of the illustration shows the 5 entered in larger size and a shaded background to highlight it.

And now, although we now have two occurrences of the digit 5 in this first vertical section group, we can*not* enter a 5 anywhere in the bottom section. We do not have the other sections in the bottom horizontal section group printed (in the illustration), which we need to make a decision. If the complete puzzle were available, we could *possibly* make a decision in this section.

Situation C: Multiple Available Cells Spanning Multiple Rows or Columns or Both

Another example is appropriate when you have multiple empty cells spanning multiple rows or columns or both within the section in which you seek to enter a digit.

Look at illustration 5. You are working the first horizontal section group with the digit 2. You see the 2 occupying S3R2C7. Look back to section 1 (with row 2 now eliminated), and you see five empty cells, three of which could possibly contain the digit 2 (S1R1C1, S1R1C2, and S1R3C3). Scanning C1, we find a 2 in S4R5C1, which automatically eliminates C1 (and cell S1R1C1). With two empty cells now available in S1

		6		3	1		4	
9				6	7	2	5	
1	5		8			6		7
	9	3						
2		5						
7								
		9						
3		1						
		4						

A. puzzle after Technique 3

		6		3	1		4	
9				6	7	2	5	
1	5	2	8			6		7

B. Puzzle with digit 2 solved

Illustration 5: with multiple cells available spanning multiple rows and columns.

(S1R1C2 and S1RC3), we cannot solve section 1 until we eliminate one of the cells! Thus we will focus on section 7.

Remember, we have a 2 given in C1, so S7C1 is automatically eliminated. In S7C3, all three cells are already filled with existing digits, and thus C3 is also eliminated. Therefore (and I will say it two ways), in S7, you can enter a 2 only in C2, so obviously C2 is *eliminated* from the 2 in S1, or with the three cells in S7C3 already filled with digits, you can enter a 2 only in S7C2.

Looking again at S1, both R1C1 and 2, and R2. have been eliminated from use by a 2; therefore, you can enter the digit 2 only in S1R3C3.

The bottom part of illustration 4 shows the top horizontal group only with the 2 entered in larger print and a shaded cell for increased visibility. It's time now for a working exercise, and we will continue with our sample puzzle 1, which we have worked on thus far but which is not yet completed.

Working Exercise 8

Using your sample 1 puzzle which you have been working thus far in this tutorial, continue to solve it with technique 4.

Begin with the top, first horizontal section group, and the digit 1 (increasing it through 9). Remember, we are now scanning the sections for a *pair* of digits *or* (a very important "or") a *single* digit and solving them with appropriate actions from the situations in this technique or previous techniques. I will write only the positive digits that have an action to perform; I will omit listing every digit 1 through 9, but you will double-check every digit. Right?

Digit 4 is a single digit occurring in S2R1C6. Scanning S3, you see that there are two empty cells in R2C7 and 9 and that S3R3 already have the three cells occupied. C9 already has a 4 in S9;

therefore S3R2C7 is the only cell in which you can correctly enter a 4. Enter a 4 there.

Now with a pair of the digit 4 in the top horizontal section group, focus on S1 and R3, which is missing a 4; S1R3C2 is the only empty cell in S1R3, so enter the 4 there.

Digit 6 is a single digit in S1R3C3. S2 has two cells available (for the digit 6) so we cannot make an entry there now. S3R2 has only one empty cell in S3R2, which needs a 6. Enter a 6 in S3R2C9.

Again, with two occurrences of the digit 6 in the top horizontal section group (S1 and 3, R2 and 3), we can return to S2 and technique 1. S2R1 needs a 6, and there is only one empty cell in S2R1. Enter the 6 in S2R1C5.

Digit 8 is a single digit in the horizontal section group in S3R3C8. Looking at S2, R1 is complete and has no cell available for an 8, and R3 is eliminated from having the digit 8 because the 8 already occurs in S3R3. Therefore, S2R2 has only one empty cell available for the digit 8. Enter an 8 in S2R2C5. (Did you double-check the column?)

Although we now have a pair of 8s in the top horizontal section group, we cannot solve the location of the third 8 in the section group because there are two empty cells in S1R1 and there is no 8 is in either intersecting column of S1R1 (C1 and 3). No decision can be made as to which cell is correct.

Digit 9 occurs in only a single cell, in S3R2C8. In S2R3C4 and 5 are two empty cells; the intersecting column, S5R5C5, already has the digit 9, which eliminates C5. That leaves S2R3C4 as the correct cell in which to enter a 9. Enter a 9 in S2R3C4. We cannot resolve the location in S1 for the 9 because there is no 9 in either intersecting column.

Move your focus down to the second horizontal section group.

There is a pair of the digit 4 in S4 and 5, R1 and 3 and it can be solved now. We had just entered a 4 in S3R2C7, which leaves S6R5C8 available for the digit 4. Enter a 4 in S6R5C8.

Digit 8 is given in S6R5C9. Looking at S5, two empty cells are S5R4C6 and S5R6C4; the cell S5R4C6 is eliminated by the intersecting column, which has an 8 in S8R9C6. That leaves S5R6C4 available for the digit 8, so enter the 8 there.

We now have a pair of the digit 8 with S4 needing an 8. R5 and 6 are eliminated, but there are two empty cells in S4R4 C1 and 2. C2 has an 8 in S7R7C2, so column 2 is also eliminated. That leaves S4R4C1 as the only available empty cell for the digit 8; enter it there.

There are two occurrences of the digit 9 in our section group in S5 and 6, R5 and 6. That leaves one cell available in R4, S4R4C2, for the digit 9. Enter the 9 in S4R4C2.

Focus now on the bottom, or third, horizontal section group.

Digit 6 is a single cell digit in S8R7C4. Look right to S9. R7 is eliminated by the 6 in S8. R9 is also eliminated, as all three cells are already filled in that section. That leaves only S9R8C8 as available for the digit 6. Enter the 6 in S9R8C8.

There are now the two occurrences of the digit 6 in horizontal section group 3. S7R9 needs a 6, as R7 and 8 are eliminated. Cells S7R9C2 and 3 are available for the digit 6, but C3 is eliminated because of the 6 occurring in S1R3C3. So enter the digit 6 in S7R9C2.

Digit 9 is a single cell digit in S9R7C7. Looking left to S8, R9C4 is eliminated because of the 9 in S2R3C4, so enter the digit 9 in S8R8C6.

With two occurrences of the digit 9 in our section group, it leaves only S7R9C3 for the digit 9; enter it there.

We have finished the scans of all three horizontal groups. Now, we are ready to go on to working exercise 9 and scan the vertical section groups.

Working Exercise 9

Continue working the sample 1 puzzle, and it will be finished in this exercise.

Begin with the leftmost, or first, vertical section group, and the digit 1 (increasing it by 1 through 9); scan the sections for a pair of digits, *or* a single digit, and solve them with the appropriate actions from this technique or previous techniques.

Digit 3 is a single digit cell in S4R6C3. Scanning down to S7, one cell remains, S7R8C1. Enter the digit 3 there. We now have two occurrences of digit 3 in this section group. S1 needs a 3; and with C1 and 3 eliminated, only one cell remains empty in C2; enter the digit 3 in S1R2C2.

Digit 6 has two occurrences in S1 and 7 and C3 and 2; both sections and rows are eliminated. The only cell empty in S4 is S4R6C1; enter a 6 in S4R6C1.

Digit 8 has two occurrences in S4 and 7 and C1 and 2. Enter the digit 8 in S1R1C3, which is the only cell available for the 8.

Digit 9 has two occurrences in S4 and 7 and C2 and 3. The digit 9 can only be entered in cell S1R1C1, and that is the only empty cell in S1.

Move your focus right to the second, or middle, vertical section group. Scan again for digits 1 through 9.

Digit 3 is a single digit cell in S5R5C6. C4 has only one empty cell, and needs a 3 in S8R9C4. Enter the digit 3 in S8R9C4. Now with two occurrences of the digit 3, S2R3C5 is the only empty cell for it. Enter the 3 in S2R3C5.

Digit 6 has two occurrences in our section group, with S5R4C6 as the only empty cell. Enter the digit 6 in S5R4C6.

Move your focus right to the third, or rightmost, vertical section group, and scan again 1 through 9.

Digit 3 is a pair. S9R7C8 is empty and requires the digit 3. Enter it there.

Digit 6 is a pair. S6R5C7 is empty and requires the digit 6. Enter it there.

And we have completed the sample puzzle 1 with my four techniques. I hope it was *fun* and *exciting* for you. I also hope you developed some skills with which you will solve many other puzzles.

Master the four previous techniques. With them, you should be able to solve 99 percent of the very-easy- and easy-rated puzzles. The techniques will also solve *many* medium-rated puzzles and a *few hard*-rated ones.

At this time, I strongly suggest that you solve the sample puzzles 2 and 3 (See appendix, illustration 11) for practice. Keep this tutorial handy and follow each technique in sequence. Get started and *try*. Also, build your skills by solving *many* other puzzles in the newsstand publications.

Parts 2 and 3 follow with advanced techniques, but get your good foundation and some experience before going on.

PART 2
Intermediate Level

Technique 5: Solving One and Two Empty Cells

Solving One and Two Empty Cells

Note—a "work area" is simply the portion of the puzzle that will be affected by the digit you enter and the location of the cell in which you entered it. From the rules of sudoku, the work area may be a row, a column, or a section, each of which can have only one occurrence of each digit 1 through 9.

Do not be confused. Every single cell in the puzzle can contain only one digit, but it is counted in all three of the work areas (i.e., the section, the row, and the column).

Note 2—this technique is is the only technique in part 2, all by itself, because the actions in this technique can and will be used independently and repeatedly at various times as you work techniques 3 through 7. Also you may see an opportunity to use it only in any single section, row or column (i.e. only in a part of the puzzle) while you are solving the puzzle. Do not be afraid to use it after you have gained significant experience by using all of the techniques in their entirety.

Start simple by searching for one work area that has *only one* empty cell.

Scan each row (top to bottom) for a row that has only one empty cell. Then scan the completed cells in that row for the entered digits 1 through 9. One digit will be missing; enter the missing digit in the empty cell. Continue your scan for the next row with one empty cell, and repeat this paragraph until you have scanned all nine rows.

Scan each column (left to right) for a column that has only one empty cell. Then scan the completed cells in that column for the entered digits 1 through 9. One digit will be missing; enter the missing digit in the empty cell. Continue your scan for the next column with one empty cell, and repeat this paragraph until you have scanned all nine columns.

Scan each section (1 through 9) for a section that has only one empty cell. Then scan the completed cells in that section for the entered digits 1 through 9. One digit will be missing; enter the missing digit in the empty cell. Continue your scan for the next section with one empty cell, and repeat this paragraph until you have scanned all nine sections.

Repeat the previous three paragraphs (scans of row, column, and section) until you no longer find one with an empty cell.

Search work areas for ones that have two empty cells.

Scan the rows for a row with two empty cells. When you find one, scan the completed cells in the row for the two missing digits 1 through 9; remember the two missing digits.

Choose either one of the missing digits. I will identify the digit you chose as the "first digit" and the other missing digit as the "second digit"; remember this identification for the following instructions.

Scan the intersecting columns of both empty cells for the first digit. If you do not find your first digit in either column, you cannot determine which of the two empty cells in the row should have that first digit.

Then, using the second digit, repeat the scan of the two intersecting columns of both empty cells for the second digit. If you do not find your second digit in either column, you cannot determine which of the two empty cells in the row should have that second digit. At this point, you will have to leave these empty cells empty and continue your scan for the next row with two empty cells.

However, if you did find the first digit in either column, that column (the one with the occurrence of the first digit) is eliminated for that first digit. Thus enter the second digit in the cell in the original row that intersects the column (i.e., the column that was eliminated by containing the first digit), and enter the first digit in the other empty cell in the row.

And the *same* action is correct if you found the second digit in either column.

Note—it is possible in the first iterations of this procedure that you may not find either digit in either row.

Continue scanning the rows for the next one with two empty cells, and repeat this procedure.

Next, scan the columns for a column with two empty cells. When you find one, scan the completed cells in the column for the two missing digits 1 through 9; remember the two missing digits.

Choose either one of the missing digits. I will identify the digit you chose as the first digit, and the other missing digit will be identified as the second digit; remember this identification for the following instructions.

Scan the intersecting rows of both empty cells for the first digit. If you do not find your first digit in either row, you cannot determine which of the two empty cells in the column should have that first digit.

Therefore, using the second digit, repeat the scan of the two intersecting rows of both empty cells for the second digit. If you do not find your second digit in either row, you cannot determine which of the two empty cells in the column should have that second digit. At this point, you will have to leave these empty cells empty and go on to the next column with two empty cells.

However, if you did find the first digit in either row, that row (the one with the occurrence of the first digit) is eliminated for that first digit. Thus, enter the second digit in the cell in the original column that intersects the row (i.e., the row that was eliminated by containing the first digit), and then enter the first digit in the other empty cell.

And the same action is correct if you found the second digit in either row.

Note—it is possible in the first iterations of this procedure that you may not find either digit in either column. (An example of this is in working exercise 10.)

Continue scanning the columns for the next column with two empty cells, and repeat this procedure.

When we come to sections, our focus is primarily the digit. Scan each section (1 through 9) for two empty cells. For any section with two empty cells, scan the section for the missing two digits, and remember the digits. Using either one of the digits, choose either one of the empty cells, and then scan (cross-check) both the intersecting row *and* column for the digit.

If you find that digit in either the row or column, that digit is eliminated from the cell in the section. You must enter the other digit in the chosen cell. Your first digit will then go in the second empty cell.

Otherwise, if you do not find that digit in either the row or column, you must enter that digit in the chosen empty cell. The second, unused, digit will then go in the other empty cell.

For every digit I enter in this technique, I double-check the rules of sudoku (each and every section, row, and column must have one and only one occurrence of each digit 1 through 9). If there is an infraction, you know you made a mistake sometime previously; it must be corrected or the puzzle reworked before you go on.

Now it is time for the working exercise.

Working Exercise 10

Note—you must use illustration 6 and work it as you do this working exercise. I created this illustration specifically for this technique; and have solved it through technique 4.

2		8		4		7	6	
		4	2	7	6	8	3	
9	7	6	8			4	5	2
3	2	7		9	8	5	4	6
6	8		4			2	9	7
4	9		7	6	2	3	1	8
7	6			8	5		2	4
8	5	2	6		4		7	3
	4	9		2	7	6	8	5

Illustration 6 was created by author to
work Technique 5.

Scan the puzzle for rows that have one empty cell. You find the first one in R4, cell S5R4C4. Scan row 4 for the missing digit; remember the rules of sudoku that *each* row must have one and only one occurrence of each digit 1 through 9. Immediately, you do *not* see a digit 1 in row 4; double-check row 4 for all the other digits (1 through 9), and you are OK to enter a 1 in the cell S5R4C4.

Continue your scan for another row with one empty cell. Did you find it? It is in R6, cell S4R6C3. Scan the entire row for the missing digit. Yes, the digit 5 is missing, so enter it in the cell.

There are no more rows with one empty cell. Scan the columns for only one empty cell.

There are none. So you must work the rows with only two empty cells. Begin at the top, and scan the rows.

The first one you find is row 3 and columns 5 and 6. Scan the row for the two missing digits. They are 1 and 3. Scan both of the intersecting columns. We do not find either a 1 or 3 in either column. Thus, we conclude that either digit could be entered in either column. So we can*not* decide into which of these two empty cells to enter either digit correctly and uniquely. We will have to wait for a later iteration after we have solved other rows or columns. *(Do not guess or force an entry!)*

Continue your scan down to the next occurrence at row 8, columns 5 and 7. Scan the row for the two missing digits—1 and 9, right? Scan both of the intersecting columns for either a 1 or 9. Column 5 has a 9 already in S5R4C5; therefore, the 9 is eliminated from C5. That leaves the other missing digit, the 1, as the only correct entry for S8R8C5. Thus the 9 must be entered in cell S9R8C7 to complete our row.

Continue your scan down for another row with two empty cells. Row 9 has two empty cells in columns 1 and 4. Scan the row for the missing digits. They are 1 and 3. A scan of the intersecting vertical column (C1) shows a 3 in column 1 (S4R4C1); thus 3 is eliminated from S7R9C1, forcing us to enter the 1 in S7R9C1. And that leaves us to correctly enter the 3 in S8R9C4. That completes that row. But double-check it to be sure.

Since you are a rational, thinking human, remember we left row 3 incomplete. But because we have now solved several cells since leaving row 3, we should revisit it; maybe it can be solved now. Remember, the missing digits in row 3 were 1 and 3, and the empty cells were C5 and 6. When we entered the 1 in S8R8C5 previously, the digit 1 was eliminated from entry in column 5 and specifically from cell S2R3C5. Thus the 3 is the only correct entry in S2R3C5; that leaves the digit 1 to be entered in S2R3C6. But again double-check these entries against the three rules of sudoku for accuracy.

Working Exercise 11

All the rows with one and two empty cells are now solved.

We will turn our attention to columns. There is a situation that will redirect our attention *from* columns *to* sections and then rows *and back to* columns. Just fasten your seat belt and hold on, remembering the basic three rules of sudoku.

Scan the columns for one or two empty cells. We will look for either with one pass.

Column 1 has only a single empty cell in S1R2C1. Scanning the column, we determine the missing digit is 5, which can be entered now in S1R2C1.

Continue to the right, and column 2 has two empty cells. Scan the column for two missing digits. They are 1 and 3. Starting at the top, scan the intersecting row (R1). We do not find either digit. Not knowing which digit to enter in S1R1C2, we will scan row 2, which has the other empty cell. Our scan for the missing digits in the column (which are 1 and 3) in row 2 reveals that the digit 3 already occupies that row in S3R2C8, which forces the 1 to be entered in S1R2C2, and that returns us to row 1, where we must enter the 3 in S1R1C2.

Moving on to the right, column 3 has two empty cells, and the missing digits are 1 and 3. Since the digits 1 and 3 do not exist in either row, we cannot eliminate either digit from either cell in our column; thus, we received no help by scanning the rows. But *wait*! *Stop!* Remember I said we would be redirected to sections, to rows, and back. Well, here we are! (I call this letting the puzzle guide our actions, not any rigid techniques.)

Look at cell S4R5C3. It is the only empty cell in the section. Scanning the digits in section 4, we find the missing digit is 1; enter 1 in S4R5C3. Likewise, the other empty cell in C3 is S7R7C3; it also is a single cell in the section (and column, now). Our missing digit in the section and row is a 3. Then enter the 3 in S7R7C3. Column solved!

Before we return to working columns, let your eyes shift focus from the section to the row. Right next door (to the right), S8R7C4 is a single empty cell in the section. The missing digit in the section is 9. Enter it in the empty cell.

Three more columns right, we have another single empty cell in S9R7C7. Scan the section for the missing digit. It is 1. Although the missing digit is 1 in the section, I continue double checking the digits in sequence 1 through 9 in the row and column. Okay, enter the 1 in the cell S9R7C7.

Return to scanning the columns. Remember, we were scanning column 3 when we left the column. Moving right, we now focus on column 4.

Column 4 now has only a single empty cell, S1R1C4. The scan of column 4 reveals the column is missing digit 5. Enter it. Take a minute and look at column 4; when we started this technique, column 4 had *four* empty cells, and we have solved all of them!

If you have worked along with me this far and have learned what we have done, I believe you could finish this puzzle without further help. But I will still finish it for you in this tutorial. Continue with me.

Move right one column; we find one empty cell in S5R5C5. The missing digit is 5, so enter the 5 in S5R5C5.

Move right to the next column, and we have two empty cells in column 6, in rows 1 and 5. At this point, *both* sections 2 and 5 each have only one empty cell. Scanning section 2 *(not the row)*, the missing digit is 9; enter a 9 in S2R1C6. In section 5, the missing digit is 3, by scanning either the section or rcolumn. Enter the 3 in S5R5C6.

Now move right to the last column (C9), as there are no empty cells in C7 and 8. There are two empty cells in C9, S3R1C9 and S3R2C9, with the missing digits 1 and 9. The scan of the rows shows the missing digit in row 1 is a 1. Enter a 1 in S3R1C9. And in row 2, the missing digit is a 9; enter the digit 9 in S3R2C9.

And the puzzle is *done*! Did you count that we entered twenty-one digits in this illustration in this one technique. There was a lot of work and reason (thought) involved.

PART 3
Advanced Procedures

Technique 6: Determining Penciled Candidate Lists

Technique 7: Solving the Penciled Candidate Lists

(Including Advanced Procedures)

Conclusion: Self-Check Your Work

File Nbr
DO1116
203H
After T5

Solver
rlw

Date Began
4/1/17

Date
Completed

Work Check

Ans Check

2		1						5
		3						
4		9						
								9
				5		8		
1		6		9		7		
							1	
		4		7				6

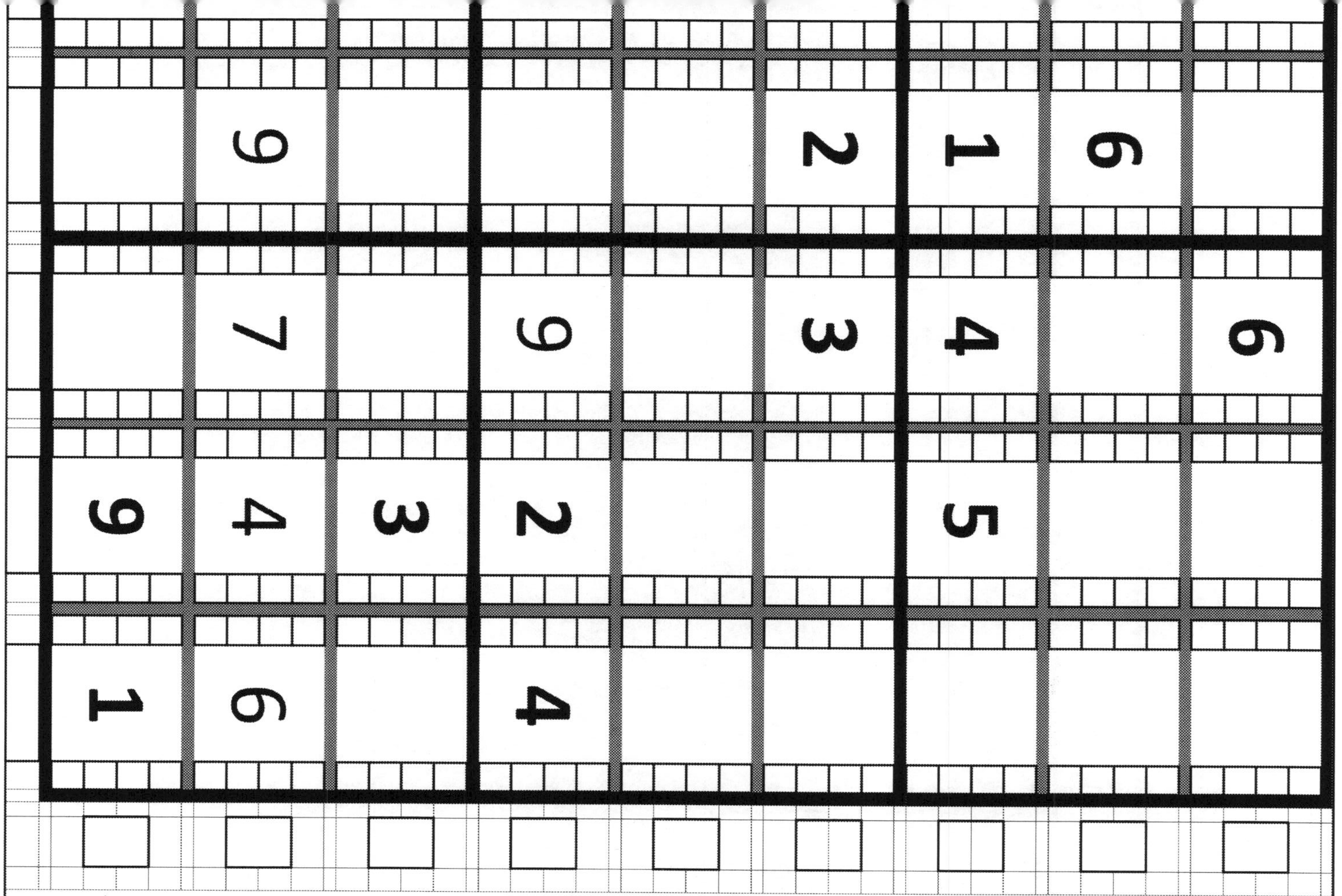

Illustration 7: Sample puzzle 4 solved ready for Technique 6.

Determining Penciled Candidate Lists

Note—sample puzzle 4 will be used in part 3. It is a hard-rated puzzle, but do not worry for I will take you step by step to the finish. I have worked it through technique 5 (see parts 1 and 2) and saved a copy of it at that point as illustration 7, which is included in this tutorial (prior page). As you can see, with a hard-rated puzzle, very few cells can be solved through technique 5. Nonetheless, this is where the fun and challenge begins, and it is here that we begin this technique 6.

I have designed (and used for two or three years) a special layout with sidebars in each cell so that you can enter the individual candidate digits (1 through 9) every time in the *same* location in every empty cell. (See appendix, illustration 13, for a blank copy of it; you may copy it for your personal use only or create your own version using Microsoft Office Excel (which is what I did). I use the left sidebar locations for the digits 1 through 4, top to bottom, and the right sidebar locations for the digits 6 through 9. I place the digit 5 in the lower left corner inside the cell. I have found that the consistent positional placement of the candidate digits is very helpful, as it reduces the time spent searching candidate lists when solving the cells.

Technique 6, determining penciled candidate lists, relies entirely on the basic rules of sudoku (each and every row, column, and section must have one and only one occurrence of each digit

1 through 9). Therefore, the procedure for entering the penciled candidate lists is to work each empty cell in the puzzle (after having worked it through all the techniques 1 through 5). When you work an empty cell, begin with the digit 1 (increasing it through 9) and scan the row, column, and section where that cell is located. If that digit already exists in any one of the three work areas, it is *not* a candidate for that cell; increase the digit and scan again. If your digit does *not* exist in any one of the work areas, it is a candidate for that cell; enter it in the appropriate small square in the sidebars. You will often enter the same digit in the candidate lists in multiple cells. This is normal, and will be resolved in technique 7.

It is extremely important and worthwhile to double-check to be absolutely sure your candidate lists are accurate and are kept up-to-date while penciling and solving the candidate lists. I do not know how many puzzles I have solved during which I was temporarily stuck (and often for extended, wasted periods of time and frustration) until I saw an error I had made in the accuracy of the candidate lists.

I choose to begin penciling candidates by working sections (in sequence 1 to 9); in the sample puzzle, I start with cell S1R1C3. When you work your other puzzles, you may choose a different starting point (e.g., work rows top to bottom or a section with the fewest empty cells). However, since the procedure is the same (scan the section, row, and column), we should always end up with *exactly* the same candidate lists.

We are ready to start the working exercises.

___

Working Exercise 12

Using illustration 7, we will begin with section 1. Again, I repeat the rules: each row, column, and section must contain one and only one occurrence of each digit 1 through 9; scan every work area (section, row, and column). If you do *not* find an occurrence of the digit, it is a candidate for that cell. A single occurrence of the digit in any *one* work area will disqualify it from that cell's candidate list. For consistency and assurance I have been thorough by using the algorithm of the sequence of section, row and column (SRC) when checking all other cells before entering a candidate. Although any one occurrence will disqualify the digit from the candidate list, I will complete and list the full algorithm.

Cell S1R1C3

Digit 1 occurs in section.

Digit 2 occurs in section.

Digit 3 occurs in section.

Digit 4 is *not* found in any work area; enter the digit 4 in the bottom position in the left sidebar.

Digit 5 occurs in row and column.

Digit 6 occurs in row.

Digit 7 occurs in column.

Digit 8 is *not* found in any work area; enter the digit in position 3 in the right sidebar.

Digit 9 occurs in column.

Cell S1R2C1

Digit 1 occurs in section and column.

Digit 2 occurs in section.

Digit 3 occurs in section.

Digit 4 occurs in column.

Digit 5 is *not* found in any work area; enter the digit in position in the lower left corner inside the cell.

Digit 6 occurs in row.

Digit 7 is *not* found in any work area; enter the digit in position 2 in the right sidebar.

Digit 8 is *not* found in any work area; enter the digit in position 3 in the right sidebar.

Digit 9 is *not* found in any work area; enter the digit in the bottom position in the right sidebar.

Cell S1R2C2

Digit 1 occurs in section.

Digit 2 occurs in section.

Digit 3 occurs in section.

Digit 4 occurs in column.

Digit 5 is *not* found in any work area; enter the digit in position in the lower left corner inside the cell.

Digit 6 occurs in row and column.

Digit 7 is *not* found in any work area; enter the digit in position 2 in the right sidebar.

Digit 8 is *not* found in any work area; enter the digit in position 3 in the right sidebar.

Digit 9 occurs in column.

Cell S1R2C3

Digit 1 occurs in section.

Digit 2 occurs in section.

Digit 3 occurs in section.

Digit 4 is *not* found in any work area; enter the digit in bottom position in the left sidebar.

Digit 5 occurs in column.

Digit 6 occurs in row.

Digit 7 occurs in column.

Digit 8 is *not* found in any work area; enter the digit in position 3 in the right sidebar.

Digit 9 occurs in column.

Cell S1R3C1

Digit 1 occurs in section, row and column.

Digit 2 occurs in section.

Digit 3 occurs in section.

Digit 4 occurs in row and column.

Digit 5 occurs in row.

Digit 6 is *not* found in any work area; enter the digit in the top position in the right sidebar.

Digit 7 is *not* found in any work area; enter the digit in position 2 in the right sidebar.

Digit 8 is *not* found in any work area; enter the digit in position 3 in the right sidebar.

Digit 9 is *not* found in any work area; enter the digit in the bottom position in the right sidebar.

Cell S1R3C3

Digit 1 occurs in section and row.

Digit 2 occurs in section.

Digit 3 occurs in section.

Digit 4 occurs in row.

Digit 5 occurs in row and column.

Digit 6 is *not* found in any work area; enter the digit in the top position in the right sidebar.

Digit 7 occurs in column.

Digit 8 is *not* found in any work area; enter the digit in position 3 in the right sidebar.

Digit 9 occurs in column.

We have completed the candidate list in section 1 together.

Working Exercise 13

Cell S2R1C4

Digit 1 occurs in section, row and column.

Digit 2 occurs in row.

Digit 3 is *not* found in any work area; enter the digit in position 3 in the left sidebar.

Digit 4 is not found in any work area; enter the digit in the bottom position in the left sidebar.

Digit 5 occurs in section row.

Digit 6 occurs in section and row.

Digit 7 occurs in column.

Digit 8 occurs in column.

Digit 9 is *not* found in any work area; enter the digit in the bottom position in right sidebar.

Cell S2R1C6

Digit 1 occurs in section and row.

Digit 2 occurs in row and column.

Digit 3 is *not* found in any work area; enter the digit in position 3 in the left sidebar.

Digit 4 is *not* found in any work area; enter the digit in the bottom position in the left sidebar.

Digit 5 occurs in section.

Digit 6 occurs in section and row.

Digit 7 is *not* found in any work area; enter the digit in position 2 in the right sidebar.

Digit 8 is *not* found in any work area; enter the digit in position 3 in the right sidebar.

Digit 9 occurs in column.

Cell S2R2C4

Digit 1 occurs in section and column.

Digit 2 is *not* found in any work area; enter the digit in position 2 in the left sidebar.

Digit 3 is *not* found in any work area; enter the digit in position 3 in the left sidebar.

Digit 4 is *not* found in any work area; enter the digit in the bottom position in the left sidebar.

Digit 5 occurs in section.

Digit 6 occurs in section.

Digit 7 occurs in column.

Digit 8 occurs in column.

Digit 9 is *not* found in any work area; enter the digit in the bottom position in the right sidebar.

Cell S2R2C5

Digit 1 occurs in section.

Digit 2 is *not* found in any work area; enter the digit in position 2 in the left sidebar.

Digit 3 is *not* found in any work area; enter the digit in position 3 in the left sidebar.

Digit 4 is *not* found in any work area; enter the digit in the bottom position in the left sidebar.

Digit 5 occurs in section.

Digit 6 occurs in section and column.

Digit 7 is *not* found in any work area; enter the digit in position 2 in the right sidebar.

Digit 8 is *not* found in any work area; enter the digit in position 3 in the right sidebar.

Digit 9 occurs in column.

Cell S2R3C4

Digit 1 occurs in section and column.

Digit 2 is *not* found in any work area; enter the digit in position 2 in the left sidebar.

Digit 3 occurs in row.

Digit 4 occurs in row.

Digit 5 occurs in section and row.

Digit 6 occurs in section.

Digit 7 occurs in column.

Digit 8 occurs in column.

Digit 9 is *not* found in any work area; enter the digit in the bottom position in the right sidebar.

Cell S2R3C5

Digit 1 occurs in section.

Digit 2 is *not* found in any work area; enter the digit in position 2 in the left sidebar.

Digit 3 occurs in row.

Digit 4 occurs in row.

Digit 5 occurs in section and row.

Digit 6 occurs in section and column.

Digit 7 is *not* found in any work area; enter the digit in position 2 in the right sidebar.

Digit 8 is *not* found in any work area; enter the digit in position 3 in the right sidebar.

Digit 9 occurs in column.

Working Exercise 14

Cell S3R1C8

Digit 1 occurs in row.

Digit 2 occurs in row and column.

Digit 3 occurs in column.

Digit 4 occurs in section and column.

Digit 5 occurs in section and row.

Digit 6 occurs in section.

Digit 7 is *not* found in any work area; enter the digit in position 2 in the right sidebar.

Digit 8 is *not* found in any work area; enter the digit 8 in position 3 in the right sidebar.

Digit 9 occurs in column.

Cell S3R1C9

Digit 1 occurs in row.

Digit 2 occurs in row.

Digit 3 is *not* found in any work area; enter the digit in position 3 in the left sidebar.

Digit 4 occurs in section and column.

Digit 5 occurs in section and row.

Digit 6 occurs in section and column.

Digit 7 is *not* found in any work area; enter the digit in position 2 in the right sidebar.

Digit 8 is *not* found in any work area; enter the digit in position 3 in the right sidebar.

Digit 9 is *not* found in any work area; enter the digit in the bottom position in the right sidebar.

Cell S3R2C7

Digit 1 is *not* found in any work area; enter the digit in the top position in the left sidebar.

Digit 2 is *not* found in any work area; enter the digit in position 2 in the left sidebar.

Digit 3 occurs in column.

Digit 4 occurs in section.

Digit 5 occurs in section.

Digit 6 occurs in section and row.

Digit 7 occurs in column.

Digit 8 is *not* found in any work area; enter the digit in position 3 in the right sidebar.

Digit 9 occurs in column.

Cell S3R2C8

Digit 1 is *not* found in any work area; enter the digit in the top position in the left sidebar.

Digit 2 occurs in column.

Digit 3 occurs in column.

Digit 4 occurs in section and column.

Digit 5 occurs in section.

Digit 6 occurs in section and row.

Digit 7 is *not* found in any work area; enter the digit in position 2 in the right sidebar.

Digit 8 is *not* found in any work area; enter the digit in position 3 in the right sidebar.

Digit 9 occurs in column.

Cell S3R2C9

Digit 1 occurs in column.

Digit 2 is *not* found in any work area; enter the digit in position 2 in the left sidebar.

Digit 3 is *not* found in any work area; enter the digit in position 3 in the left sidebar.

Digit 4 occurs in section and column.

Digit 5 occurs in section.

Digit 6 occurs in section and column.

Digit 7: is not found in any work area; enter the digit in position 2 in right side bar.

Digit 8 is *not* found in any work area; enter the digit in position 3 in the right sidebar.

Digit 9 is *not* found in any work area; enter the digit in the bottom position in the right sidebar.

Cell S3R3C9

Digit 1 occurs in row and column.

Digit 2 is *not* found in any work area; enter the digit in position 2 in the left sidebar.

Digit 3 occurs in row.

Digit 4 occurs in section and column.

Digit 5 occurs in section.

Digit 6 occurs in section and column.

Digit 7 is *not* found in any work area; enter the digit in position 2 in the right sidebar.

Digit 8 is *not* found in any work area; enter the digit in position 3 in the right sidebar.

Digit 9 is *not* found in any work area; enter the digit in the bottom position in the right sidebar.

We have worked the full top horizontal section group, and I have explicitly used the full sequence of digits 1 through 9 for every empty cell. In the next horizontal section group, I will only show the digits you will enter in the candidate lists of the empty cells. For accuracy, practice, and the solidification of your skills, I *strongly* recommend that you scan *every* empty cell with every digit, 1 through 9, and *all* work areas (section, row, and column). However in the following exercise, I will list *only* the first work area occurrence of the digit; you do remember that any one single occurrence in any work area will disqualify the digit.

Working Exercise 15

Cell S4R4C3

Digit 1 is *not* found in any work area; enter the digit in the top position in the left sidebar.

Digit 6 is *not* found in any work area; enter the digit in the top position in the right sidebar.

Digit 8 is *not* found in any work area; enter the digit in position 3 in the right sidebar.

Cell S4R5C1

Digit 3 is *not* found in any work area; enter the digit in position 3 in the left sidebar.

Digit 6 is *not* found in any work area; enter the digit in the top position in the right sidebar.

Digit 7 is *not* found in any work area; enter the digit in position 2 in the right sidebar.

Digit 8 is *not* found in any work area; enter the digit in position 3 in the right sidebar.

Cell S4R5C2

Digit 2 is *not* found in any work area; enter the digit in position 2 in the left sidebar.

Digit 7 is *not* found in any work area; enter the digit in position 2 in the right sidebar.

Digit 8 is *not* found in any work area; enter the digit in position 3 in the right sidebar.

Cell S4R5C3

Digit 1 is *not* found in any work area; enter the digit in the top position in the left sidebar.

Digit 2 is *not* found in any work area; enter the digit in position 2 in the left sidebar.

Digit 3 is *not* found in any work area; enter the digit in position 3 in the left sidebar.

Digit 6 is *not* found in any work area; enter the digit in the top position in the right sidebar.

Digit 8 is *not* found in any work area; enter the digit in position 3 in the right sidebar.

Cell S4R6C1

Digit 3 is *not* found in any work area; enter the digit in position 3 in the left sidebar.

Digit 6 is *not* found in any work area; enter the digit in the top position in the right sidebar.

Digit 7 is *not* found in any work area; enter the digit in position 2 in the right sidebar.

Cell S4R6C2

Digit 7 is *not* found in any work area; enter the digit in position 2 in the right sidebar.

Cell S5R4C4

Digit 5 is *not* found in any work area; enter the digit in position in the lower left corner inside the cell.

Digit 6 is *not* found in any work area; enter the digit in the top position in the right sidebar.

Cell S5R4C5

Digit 1 is *not* found in any work area; enter the digit in the top position in the left sidebar.

Digit 7 is *not* found in any work area; enter the digit in position 2 in the right sidebar.

Cell S5R5C4

Digit 3 is *not* found in any work area; enter the digit in position 3 in the left sidebar.

Digit 4 is *not* found in any work area; enter the digit in the bottom position in the left sidebar.

Digit 5 is *not* found in any work area; enter the digit in position in the lower left corner inside the cell.

Digit 6 is *not* found in any work area; enter the digit in the top position in the right sidebar.

Cell S5R5C6

Digit 3 is *not* found in any work area; enter the digit in position 3 in the left sidebar.

Digit 4 is *not* found in any work area; enter the digit in the bottom position in the left sidebar.

Digit 5 is *not* found in any work area; enter the digit in position in the lower left corner inside the cell.

Digit 7 is *not* found in any work area; enter the digit in position 2 in the right sidebar.

Cell S5R6C5

Digit 1 is *not* found in any work area; enter the digit in the top position in the left sidebar.

Digit 3 is *not* found in any work area; enter the digit in position 3 in the left sidebar.

Digit 7 is *not* found in any work area; enter the digit in position 2 in the right sidebar.

Cell S5R6C6

Digit 3 is *not* found in any work area; enter the digit in position 3 in the left sidebar.

Digit 7 is *not* found in any work area; enter the digit in position 2 in the right sidebar.

Cell S6R4C8

Digit 1 is *not* found in any work area; enter the digit in the top position in the left sidebar.

Digit 6 is *not* found in any work area; enter the digit in the top position in the right sidebar.

Digit 7 is *not* found in any work area; enter the digit in position 2 in the right sidebar.

Digit 8 is *not* found in any work area; enter the digit in position 3 in the right sidebar.

Cell S6R4C9

Digit 5 is *not* found in any work area; enter the digit in position in the lower left corner inside the cell.

Digit 7 is *not* found in any work area; enter the digit in position 2 in the right sidebar.

Digit 8 is *not* found in any work area; enter the digit in position 3 in the right sidebar.

Cell S6R5C7

Digit 1 is *not* found in any work area; enter the digit in the top position in the left sidebar.

Digit 5 is *not* found in any work area; enter the digit in position in the lower left corner inside the cell.

Digit 8 is *not* found in any work area; enter the digit in position 3 in the right sidebar.

Cell S6R5C8

Digit 1 is not found in any work area; enter the digit in the top position in the left sidebar.

Digit 6 is *not* found in any work area; enter the digit in the top position in the right sidebar.

Digit 7 is *not* found in any work area; enter the digit in position 2 in the right sidebar.

Digit 8 is *not* found in any work area; enter the digit in position 3 in the right sidebar.

Cell S6R5C9

Digit 5 is *not* found in any work area; enter the digit in position in the lower left corner inside the cell.

Digit 7 is *not* found in any work area; enter the digit in position 2 in the right sidebar.

Digit 8 is *not* found in any work area; enter the digit in position 3 in the right sidebar.

We have penciled the candidates in the two horizontal section groups together. I do not have a second puzzle for you to practice your new skills. I hope you have learned the process now, so I will let you finish penciling the candidate lists in the last horizontal section group on your own. Remember, for every empty cell, scan for the digits 1 through 9 in every section, row, and column; if it already exists, you cannot use it in the candidate list.

Working Exercise 16

I strongly believe you must try your own skills now. Finish the third horizontal section by penciling the correct candidate lists in all the empty cells.

Do not worry or get frustrated. I have included a copy of our sample puzzle 4 with the penciled candidate lists completed, so you can check your work. (See illustration 8.)

If you have made a mistake, try to correct it. IF you do not succeed in correcting it, simply throw your puzzle 4 away, and start this technique 6 over again.

With a correct candidate list, you are ready to go on to technique 7.

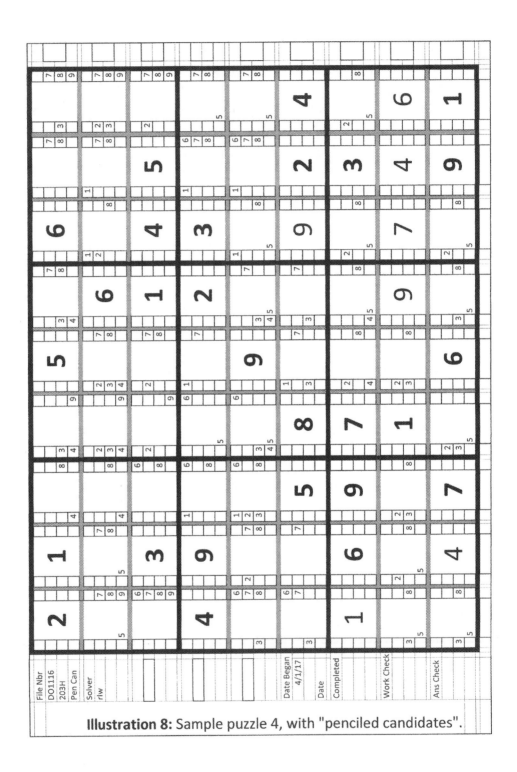

Illustration 8: Sample puzzle 4, with "penciled candidates".

Solving the Candidate Lists

As we start technique 7, there are four new actions, procedures, or situations that we often perform in solving our penciled candidates. I will discuss each of them here; then as we solve the candidate lists and find examples of each, I will give more detail. Before you enter any digit into a cell, a quick double check of the section, row, and column for any other occurrence of that digit is worthwhile and often prevents errors of having two occurrences of the same digit in a work area. These actions are:

- cleanup
- sole candidates and hidden sole candidates
- doubles and hidden doubles
- number claiming

Cleanup

When you begin solving the penciled candidate lists you created and *enter* a digit in a cell, you must clean up every time. This process is new at this point in working Sudoku puzzles and its purpose is to make sure you keep your candidate lists complete, accurate, and up-to-date. It *must* be used with every digit you enter. Once you have entered a digit into a cell, no *other* cell in the section, row, or column may have the same digit. In this process, you actually delete the digit you entered in a cell from all the other candidate lists in the cell, section, row, and column.

I like to develop sequences that I can memorize and follow and make sure I have not skipped a digit or a cell in the process. The sequence I follow is composed of four steps as follows.

1. Delete *all* remaining candidates from the list of the *cell* into which you entered a digit.
2. Delete only the digit you entered into a cell from the remaining candidate lists in all the cells in the *section*. (Note—very often cleanup of a section will overlap, cleaning up a row or column, too. This is OK. Continue.)
3. Delete only the digit you entered into a cell from the remaining candidate lists in all the cells in the *row*.
4. Delete the digit you entered into a cell from the remaining candidate lists in all the cells in the *column*.

Did you see and remember the simple four-word sequence—cell, section, row, and column? I believe it is easy to remember and consequently is a guide to delete *only the correct* digits allowed. Just remember the four-word sequence—cell, section, row, and column—and the digit you entered.

Cleanup is that simple but must be used in its entirety with every digit you enter into a cell.

Sole Candidates and *Hidden* Sole Candidates

The sole candidate occurs when a cell's candidate list contains only *one* digit. It is the only digit that can be correctly entered in the cell. Because they are more easily seen, I like to start searching for them first.

A hidden sole candidate is when a single digit is found in only one cell's candidate list in any one work area (the section, row, or column) *but* is obscured, or *hidden*, by the existence of other digits in the *same* candidate list. These are much harder to see and find, but they can really help solve what digit you correctly enter in a cell.

As you enter a digit into a cell and clean up, you will often create additional sole candidates as a chain reaction, and this helps to solve other cells.

Doubles and Hidden Doubles

Because doubles have traditionally been more difficult for me to spot and solve, I have created illustration 9 to demonstrate some situations in which doubles occur. Remember you cannot *solve* cells with doubles, but you can *eliminate* a goodly number of other digits from the candidate lists.

A plain or naked double is when *two* occurrences of the same two digits occur together only in any two cells in the same work area (section, row, or column). This means that no *other* digit may be in the *same* two cells with the same two digits that *make* the naked double. Either or both digits of the double may occur in *other* cells in the work area, with additional *other* digits. *See illustration 9, top row image; the plain or naked double is the*

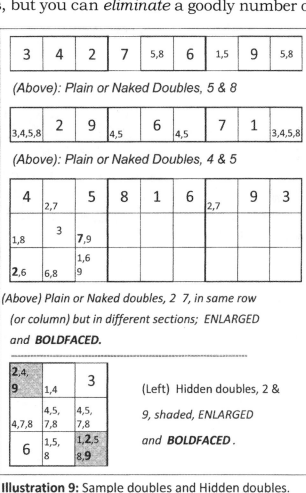

(Above): Plain or Naked Doubles, 5 & 8

(Above): Plain or Naked Doubles, 4 & 5

(Above) Plain or Naked doubles, 2 7, in same row (or column) but in different sections; ENLARGED and **BOLDFACED.**

(Left) Hidden doubles, 2 & 9, shaded, ENLARGED and **BOLDFACED** .

Illustration 9: Sample doubles and Hidden doubles.

digits 5 and 8, in cells C5 and 9. The digit 5 also occurs in C7 which can correctly be deleted leaving the digit 1 as a sole candidate which can be correctly entered in C7.

The rationale for solving a double is that each work area can have only one occurrence of each digit 1 through 9. When working a double, *if* digit #1 is entered in cell A, and the cleanup is done properly, *then* digit #2 must be entered in cell B with the cleanup action. When you entered digit #1 in cell A, you deleted digit #1 from cell B's candidate list in the cleanup and left only digit #2 in cell B as a sole candidate and vice versa. Look again at illustration 9, first row image. If you entered a 5 in C5; your cleanup deleted the 8 in C5 and the 5s in C7 and 9. This would leave the 8 as a sole candidate in C9. Digit is also a sole candidate in C7.

See illustration 9, second row image; the naked double is the digits 4 and 5 in C4 and 6. The digits 4 and 5 occur alone only in cells in C4 and 6, but both digits also occur in C1 and 9 with the additional digits 3 and 8. Delete only the digits 4 and 5 in C1 and 9 and behold, you have uncovered a second double in the row.

See working exercise 18 for an actual example of doubles.

A *hidden double* is when the exact same two digits occur only in two cells, but other numbers may occur in the same cells (and in other cells) in the work area and may obscure the double. Further, the digits (of the double) may occur singly in other cells. *See illustration 9, bottom section image; which has a hidden double, digits 2 and 9. In R1C1 the additional digit is the 4 and in R3C3 the additional digits are 1, 5, and 8. The additional digit 4 in R1C1 may be safely deleted because the digit 4 occurs in several other cells; the additional digits 1, 5, and 8 may be safely deleted from R3C3 as each of them occur in several other cells. These deletions make the empty cells in the section easier to solve (in proper time) as the section has fewer digits to work.*

Look again at illustration 9, for the third image. This part of the illustration shows a naked double with digits 2 and 7 in a row (or column) in different sections. When the cells of a double occur in different sections, you do not know which digit will eventually occupy which cell. Therefore, in the *sections* of both cells (of the double (I show only one section)) there must be at least one other occurrence of each digit. Simply stated, if the digit 2 was to be entered in C2, the digit 7 would still have to occur in another cell in the section (I.e., R2C3), and vice versus.

Note—some websites and resources add triplets and quads in this discussion. I choose to work these more complex situations (triplets and quads) down to doubles and sole candidates.

Number Claiming

The rules of sudoku are that in each section, row, and column, there can be one and *only* one occurrence of each digit 1 through 9. Number claiming is when is when a single digit occurs in two or three cells in the same row or column of a section.

The easiest ones to spot are in a section. When you examine all the candidate lists in a section and find the same digit to be only in the same row or column, that digit is claimed by that section for the entire row or column. Therefore, *that* digit cannot occur in any other cell in the row or column. If that digit is found in *another* cell in the same row or column in either of the other sections, it can be eliminated (deleted). Note the number of the occurrences of the digit is unimportant; the digit claimed may be in two, or all three cells in the section but must be in the same row or column.

There is an example of this number claiming in working exercise 22.

Some Final Words

Be prepared to solve penciled candidates all over the entire puzzle. You will *jump* around from corner to corner, edge to edge, and top to bottom, wherever the digit is found or there is a situation you can recognize and solve. There is no repeatable sequence you can follow.

The action of solving the sole candidate is used much more frequently as you near completion of the puzzle. And the number of digits to clean up (delete) greatly decreases as you solve more cells. I know you will experience this phenomenon, and it offers you *hope*!

I have included suggested checkpoints in parentheses and italics at various points in the working exercises in technique 7, solving penciled candidates. If you have copy equipment yourself, these are points at which I made a copy of the puzzle, as I solved it. When and if you get stuck and lose your way, you can go back to the last checkpoint and rework the puzzle from the last checkpoint; you will not have to go back to the beginning of the technique. And don't worry about getting stuck and lost; it will occur less and less as you gain experience.

Now, we are ready to solve the puzzle. Get your copy of the puzzle where you finished penciling the candidate lists. Let's go to the working exercises.

Working Exercise 17

I begin by looking for the simplest cells to solve and the easiest ones to find. I begin by looking for sole candidates. Do you find one in our puzzle?

In S4R6C2, there is only one candidate, the digit 7. Enter the digit 7 in cell S4R6C2, and clean up. *Since this is the first encounter we have had with an actual cleanup, I will walk you through it step by step.*

Delete all candidates from the *cell*.

The 7 is the only candidate left in this cell; delete it.

Delete the digit 7 only from every cell in section 4.

Delete only the digit 7 in cells S4R5C1, and 2, and S4R6C1.

Delete the digit 7 only from every cell in the entire row 6.

Delete only the digit 7 in S5R6C5 and 6.

Delete the digit 7 only from every cell in the entire column 2.

Delete only the digit 7 in S1R2C2.

Did you notice? Our cleanup actions created another sole candidate. In S5R6C6, the digit 3 is the sole candidate. Enter the digit 3, and clean up.

Delete all candidates from the cell.

The 3 is the only candidate left in this cell; delete it.

Delete the digit 3 only from every cell in the section 5.

Delete only the digit 3 in cells S5R5C4 and 6 and S5R6C5.

Delete the digit 3 only from every cell in the entire row 6.

Delete only the digit 3 in the cell S4R6C1.

Delete the digit 3 only from every cell in the entire column 6,.

Delete only the 3 in cells S2R1C6 and S7R9C6.

Again, a sole candidate was created in our last cleanup—not one, but two—in cells S4R6C1 and S5R6C5. In S4R6C1, the sole candidate is the digit 6. Enter the digit in cell S4R6C1, and clean up.

Delete all candidates from the cell.

The 6 is the only candidate left in this cell; delete it.

Delete the digit 6 only from every cell in section 4.

Delete only the digit 6 in cells S4R5C1 and 3 and S4R4C3.

Delete the digit 6 only from every cell in the entire row 6.

There are no 6s to delete in this row.

Delete the digit 6 only from every cell in the entire column 1.

Delete only the digit 6 in cell S1R3C1.

In S5R6C5, the sole candidate is the digit 1. Enter the digit 1 in the cell, and clean up.

Delete all candidates from the cell.

The 1 is the only candidate left in this cell; delete it.

Delete the digit 1 only from every cell in section 5.

Delete only the digit 1 in cell S5R4C5.

Delete the digit 1 only from every cell in the entire row 6.

There are no 1s to delete in this row.

Delete the digit 1 only from every cell in the entire column 5.

There are no 1s to delete in this row.

And yes, we just created one more sole candidate. There is the digit 7 as the sole candidate in S5R4C5. Enter it in the cell, and clean up. *Note that although this chain of sole candidates started with a 7, this is a different location with another digit 7 and is the end of the chain.*

Delete all candidates from the cell.

The 7 is the only candidate left in this cell; delete it.

Delete the digit 7 only from every cell in section 5.

Delete only the digit 7 in cell S5R5C6.

Delete the digit 7 only from every cell in the entire row 4.

Delete only the digit 7 in cells S6R4C8 and 9.

Delete the digit 7 only from every cell in the entire column 5.

Delete only the digit 7 in cells S2R2C5 and S2R3C5.

Oh boy! It is fun to see so many cells filling in. There were no more sole candidates created by our last cleanup.

However, before we leave this exercise, there is a hidden sole candidate in our puzzle. It is the digit 6 in cell S1R3C3. The candidate list contains the digits 6 and 8, but the digit 6 does *not* appear in any other candidate list in the section. Enter the digit 6 in cell S1R3C3, and clean up. Although this is a hidden sole candidate, the cleanup is the same process.

Delete all candidates from the cell.

Delete all the digits (both 6 and 8) from the cell, S1R3C3.

Delete from every cell in the section 1, the digit 6 only.

There are no 6s to delete in this section.

Delete from every cell in the entire row 3, the digit 6 only.

There are no 6s to delete in this row.

Delete from every cell in the entire column 3, the digit 6 only.

There are no 6s to delete in this column

(Checkpoint SA)

Working Exercise 18

I do not find any more sole candidates or hidden sole candidates. Therefore, I will go to the third action discussed at the beginning of this technique and look for doubles or hidden doubles. The first prominent one is in S1R1 and 2C3. It is a plain or naked double because both cells contain only the *same* two digits 4 and 8 and those same two digits do not occur together alone in any other cell in the work areas (i.e., the section or the column).

Warning! *Note the 4 does not occur in any other cell in the section or the column, and the digit 8 occurs in three other cells in the section and three cells in the column.* Be careful; a double can be very hard to spot and can be tricky or even deceitful, but they are necessary to work when solving sudoku. Just for instance, *if* the double had been in S1R2C1 and 2, the work areas would be the section and row (not the column). Likewise, if the double had been in S1R1C3 and S1R3C1, the work area would have been the section *only*. Further, if the double were in the same row, but in two *different* sections, the work area would be *only* the row

(See Illustration 9). *By contrast,* Look at the digits 7 and 8 in S3; they are *not* doubles. First, digits 7 and 8 occur together in more than two cells. Secondly, digits 7 and 8 occur by themselves only in cell S3R1C8; all other occurrences of the digits 7 and 8 have other digits occurring *with* them.

Now back to our double in S1R1C1 and 2; it is a clean, simple, and naked double. We cannot solve either cell of the double but we can eliminate a number of other digits. I must repeat here the logical interaction of the two cells of the double. When you enter a 4 in either cell of the double, and clean up, you leave the digit 8 as the sole candidate in the other cell and vice versus. Thus you may safely delete all *other* 4s and 8s that occur in all *other* cells in the work areas involved.

In this case, there are no other 4s to delete in the section or column.

Delete the digit 8 from all the other cells in the section.

> *Delete the digit 8 from the candidate lists in S1R2C1 and 2 and S1R3C1.*

Delete the digit 8, from all the other cells in the column.

> *Delete the digit 8 from the candidate lists in S4R4 and 5C3 and S7R8C3.*

Did you see the sole candidate we created in S4R4C3 when we deleted the 8? The sole candidate in cell S4R4C3 is the digit 1. Enter the digit in the cell, and clean up.

Delete all candidates from the cell.

> *The 1 is the only candidate left in this cell; delete it.*

Delete from every empty cell in the section 4, the digit 1 only.

Delete only the digit 1 in cell S4R5C3 in this section.

Delete from every cell in the entire row 4, the digit 1 only.

Delete only the digit 1 in cell S6R4C8 in this row.

Delete from every cell in the entire column 3, the digit 1 only.

There are no 1s to delete in this column.

There are no more entries possible as a result of the double. Thus, I will return to seeing what action I can find. I found a hidden sole candidate.

Working Exercise 19

In S2R1C6, the digit 7 is a hidden sole candidate. There is not another 7 in any empty cell in the section; this cell is the only correct cell to enter the digit 7. Enter the digit and clean up.

Delete all candidates from the cell.

Delete the digits 4, 7 and 8 from cell S2R1C6.

Delete from every empty cell in section 2, the digit 7 only.

There are no 7s to delete in this section.

Delete from every cell in the entire row 1, the digit 7 *only.*

Delete only the digit 7 in cells S3R1C8 and 9 in this row.

Delete from every cell in the entire column 6, the digit 7 only.

There are no 7s to delete in this column.

We created a sole candidate in S3R1C8 with our cleanup, the digit 8. Enter the 8, and clean up.

Delete all candidates from the cell.

The 8 is the only candidate left in this cell; delete it.

Delete from every empty cell in the section 3, the digit 8 only.

Delete only the digit 8 in cells S3R1C9, S3R2C7 8 and 9, and S3R3C9 in this section.

Delete from every cell in the entire row 1, the digit 8 only.

Delete only the digit 8 in cell S1R1C3 in this row.

Delete from every cell in the entire column 8, the digit 8 only.

Delete only the digit in cells S6R4 and 5C8 in this column.

I hope you were aware that we created two sole candidates in our cleanup. The first one involved our double in S1R1C3 (which we will solve later). The other one is in cell S6R4C8. The digit 6 is the sole candidate. Enter the digit 6, and clean up.

Delete all candidates from the cell.

The 6 is the only candidate left in this cell; delete it.

Delete from every empty cell in the section 6, the digit 6 only.

Delete only the digit 6 in cell S6R5C8 in this section.

Delete from every cell in the entire row 4, the digit 6 only.

Delete only the digit 6 in cell S5R4C4 in this row.

Delete from every cell in the entire column 8, the digit 6 only.

There are no 6s to delete in this column.

(Checkpoint SB)

Working Exercise 20

In our last cleanup, a sole candidate, a 5, was created in S5R4C4. Enter the digit 5 there, and clean up. *(Note, I am purposefully eliminating the instruction statement and writing only the action statement; I am still using the sequence of cell, section, row, and column.)*

The 5 is the only candidate left in this cell; delete it.

Delete only the digit 5 in cells S5R5C4 and 6 in this section.

Delete only the digit 5 in cell S6R4C9 in this row.

Delete only the digit 5 in cell S8R9C4 in this column.

In our last cleanup, two sole candidates were created; an 8 was created in S6R4C9, and a 4 was created in S5R5C6.

First, enter the digit 8 in S6R4C9 and clean up.

The 8 is the only candidate left in this cell; delete it.

Delete only the digit 8 in cells S6R5C7 and 9 in this section.

There are no 8s to delete in this row.

Delete only the digit 8 in cell S9R7C9 in this column.

Now, enter the digit 4 in cell S5R5C6, and clean up.

The 4 is the only candidate left in this cell; delete it.

Delete only the digit 4 in cell S5R5C4 in this section.

There are no 4s to delete in this row.

Delete only the digit 4 in cell S8R7C6 in this column.

And we just created another sole candidate; enter the digit 6 in S5R5C4, and clean up.

The 6 is the only candidate left in this cell; delete it.

There are no 6s to delete in this section, row, or column.

I hope you worked this exercise without the instruction statements; if you had trouble understanding why, I suggest you get a clean copy of the puzzle and redo technique 7 from the beginning.

(Checkpoint SC)

Working Exercise 21

I must ask if you were aware that when we entered the 8 in S6R1C8 and cleaned up the row, we modified the doubles we had in S1R1and 2C3 by deleting the 8 in cell S1R1C3, and that created a sole candidate in that cell, the 4. Enter the 4 in S1R1C3, and clean up.

The 4 is the only candidate left in this cell; delete it.

Delete only the digit 4 in cell S1R2C3 in this section.

Delete only the digit 4 in cell S2R1C4 in this row.

There are no 4s to delete in this column.

When we deleted the 4 in cell S1R2C3, we left the digit 8 (which was part of the original double) as a sole candidate in that cell. Enter the digit 8 in cell SR2C3, and clean up.

The 8 is the only candidate left in this cell; delete it.

There are no 8s to delete in this section.

Delete only the digit 8 in cell S2R2C5 in this row.

There are no 8s to delete in this column.

When we deleted the 8 in cell S2R2C5, we left a hidden sole candidate. Did you see it? In S2R3C5, the digit 8 is a hidden sole candidate. (There is no other cell in S2 with a candidate 8 in it.) So enter the digit 8 in S2R3C5, and clean up.

Delete all the candidates (the 2 and 8) left in this cell.

There are no 8s to delete in this section.

There are no 8s to delete in this row.

Delete only the digit 8 in cells S8R7 and 8C5 in this column.

Working Exercise 22

Working exercise 21 was the end of a chain. We did not create any more sole candidates in our cleanup, but I thought all the chain reactions were great! And they were a great help in solving many cells.

In this working exercise, we are going to focus on our fourth action, number claiming. The example in our sample puzzle is in S7. The number claimed by S7 is in S7R8C2 and 3, and it is the digit 2. In S7, the digit 2 occurs only in row 8 C2 and 3. It is important to take notice of that fact. Think logically, or reasonably, for a moment. S7R8C1 cannot have a digit 2! *(S1R1C1 already has the digit 2 for the entire column 1.)* Likewise, S7R9C1 cannot have a digit 2. That leaves only S7R8C2 and 3 to have the digit 2 for the section (S7); the digit 2 in S7R8C2and 3 also claims the digit 2 for the entire row (R8). Therefore we can *safely* delete all other 2s in the row. (That is value of number claiming.).

Further, we cannot determine in which of the two cells in S7R8C2 and 3 the digit 2 could be correctly be entered. Those cells cannot be solved now.

Delete only digit 2 from S8R8C5.

And that leaves the digit 3 as the sole candidate in cell S8R8C5.

Enter the digit 3 in S 8R8C5, and clean up.

> *The 3 is the only candidate left in this cell; delete it.*

> *Delete only the digit 3 in cell S8R9C4 in this section.*

> *Delete only the digit 3 in cells S7R8C1 and 3 in this row.*

> *Delete only the digit 3 in cell S2R2C5 in this column.*

Our cleanup created two more sole candidates for us, S8R9C4 and S7R8C3.

First, we will work cell S8R9C4, where the sole candidate is the digit 2. Enter the digit 2 in that cell (S8R9C4), and clean up.

The 2 is the only candidate left in this cell; delete it.

Delete only the digit 2 in cell S8R7C5 in this section.

Delete only the digit 2 in cell S9R9C7 in this row.

Delete only the digit 2 in cells S2R2C4 and S2R3C4 in this column.

We created two more sole candidates, in S8R7C5 the digit 4 and in S2R3C4 the digit 9.

We will delay action on these for now. Instead, we will work the digit 2 as the sole candidate in S7R8C3 because this cell and digit were part of our number claiming at the beginning of this exercise. While it is fresh on our minds, we need to see how number claiming works.

Enter the digit 2 in that cell (S7R8C3), and clean up.

The 2 is the only candidate left in this cell; delete it.

Delete only the digit 2 in cell S7R8C2 in this section.

There are no 2s to delete in this row.

Delete only the digit 2 in cell S4R5C3 in this column.

(Checkpoint SD)

Working Exercise 23

Although there are a number of sole candidates in our puzzle at this point, we will continue to work in S7 because it has two possible actions, which I will use to re-enforce the situation of doubles, and of hidden sole candidate.

The doubles are the digits 5 and 8 in S7R8C1 and 2; these are plain naked doubles as there is no other occurrence of only those two digits in any other cell in the section. Therefore, you *could* delete the 5 and 8 in S7R9C1 which would leave the 3 as sole candidate.

The digits 5 and 8 doubles are present in S7R8C1and 2; look also in S8 and 9. In S8R7 and 9C6 we have a 5 and 8 double. And an identical situation with the 5 – 8 double occurs in S9R7 and 9C7. Wait! The 5 – 8 double is also in R7 and 9 (spanning S8 and 9. This is a rare situation where doubles intertwine sections, rows, and columns, which all will be solved in due time.

But without acting on the on the doubles in the above paragraph, let's return to S7. The 3 in S7R9C1 is a hidden sole candidate there. The digit 3 does not exist in any other cell in the section, and the other digits in the candidate list make it hidden.

Enter the digit 3 in cell S7R9C1, and clean up.

Delete all the candidates left in this cell (digits 3, 5, and 8).

There are no 3s to delete in this section.

There are no 3s to delete in this row.

Delete only the digit 3 in cell S4R5C1 in this column.

We created a sole candidate in our last cleanup. The digit 8 is a sole candidate in cell S4R5C1. Enter the digit 8, and clean up.

The 8 is the only candidate left in this cell; delete it.

Delete only the digit 8 in cell S4R5C2 in this section.

There are no 8s to delete in this row.

Delete only the digit 8 in cell S7R8C1 in this column.

One cell (S7R8C1) of the double was solved. But a sole candidate was created in S4R5C2; the digit 2 is a sole candidate.

Enter the 2 in the cell, and clean up.

The 2 is the only candidate left in this cell; delete it.

There are no 2s to delete in this section.

There are no 2s to delete in this row.

There are no 2s to delete in this column.

S7R8C1 has a digit 5 as a sole candidate. Enter it in the cell, and clean up.

The 5 is the only candidate left in this cell; delete it.

Delete only the digit 5 in cell S7R8C2 in this section.

There are no 5s to delete in this row.

Delete only the digit 5 in cell S1R2C1 in this column.

S7R8C2 has a digit 8 as a sole candidate. Enter it in the cell, and clean up.

The 8 is the only candidate left in this cell; delete it.

There are no 8s to delete in this section.

There are no 8s to delete in this row.

There are no 8s to delete in this column.

(Checkpoint SE)

Working Exercise 24

This is exciting! The puzzle is really filling in nicely, and we are at the point where most actions are sole candidates with fewer cells to clean up. So let us continue. Let's start in the upper left corner with section 1. The first cell is S1R2C2.

Enter the 5 as a sole candidate in cell S1R2C2, and clean up.

The 5 is the only candidate left in this cell; delete it.

There are no 5s to delete in this section, row, or column.

Then in S2R3C1, the 9 is a Sole Candidate. Enter the 9 and clean-up.

The 9 is the only candidate left in this cell; delete it.

Delete only the digit 9 in cells S2R1C4 and S2R2C4 in this section.

Delete only the digit 9 in cells S1R3C1 and S3R3C9 in this row.

There are no 9s to delete in this column.

We created two sole candidates—one, a 3, in S2R1C4.

Enter the 3 in the cell, and clean up.

The 3 is the only candidate left in this cell; delete it.

Delete only the digit in cell S2R2C4 in this section.

Delete only the digit 3 in cell S3R1C9 in this row.

There are no 3s to delete in this column.

The other created sole candidate is in S1R3C1 and is the digit 7. Enter the 7 in cell S1R3C1, and clean up.

The 7 is the only candidate left in this cell; delete it.

Delete only the digit 7 in cell S1R2C1 in this section.

Delete only the digit 7 in cell S3R3C9 in this row.

There are no 7s to delete in this column.

When we cleaned up from the 3, we created a sole candidate, a 4, in S2R2C4. Enter the 4 in cell S2R2C4, and clean up.

The 4 is the only candidate left in this cell; delete it.

Delete only the digit 4 in cell S2R2C5 in this section.

There are no 4s to delete in this row.

There are no 4s to delete in this column.

Working Exercise 25

There are several more sole candidates now to work that have been delayed. Let us begin to solve them now. The first one cell is S4R5C3.

Enter the 3, as it is a sole candidate in cell S4R5C3, and clean up.

The 3 is the only candidate left in this cell; delete it.

There are no 3s to delete in this section, row, or column.

Another one is in S8R7C5, a 4. Enter the digit in in the cell, and clean up.

The 4 is the only candidate left in this cell; delete it.

There are no 4s to delete in this section, row or column.

A third one is the digit 2 in cell S2R2C5. Enter the digit 2 in the cell, and clean up.

The 2 is the only candidate left in this cell; delete it.

There are no 2s to delete in this section.

Delete only the digit 2 in cells S3R2C7 and 9 in this row.

There are no 2s to delete in column.

We created a sole candidate, a 1, in S3R2C7. Enter a 1 there, and clean up.

The 1 is the only candidate left in this cell; delete it.

Delete only the digit 1 in cell S3R2C8 in this section.

There are no 1s to delete in this row.

Delete only the digit 1 in cell S6R5C7 in this column.

We just created a sole candidate, the 7, S3R2C8. Enter the 7 in the cell, and clean up.

The 7 is the only candidate left in this cell; delete it.

Delete only the digit 7 in cell S3R2C9 in this section.

There are no 7s to delete in this row.

Delete only the digit 7 in cell S6R5C8 in this column.

We have created more sole candidates, but let's delay them, and solve the sole candidate in S1R2C1, a 9.

Enter the 9 in cell S1R2C1, and clean up.

The 9 is the only candidate left in this cell; delete it.

There are no 9s to delete in this section.

Delete only the digit 9 in cell S3R2C9 in this row.

There are no 9s to delete in this column.

(Checkpoint SF)

Working Exercise 26

All of the sole candidates in this working exercise were created earlier and action delayed until now.

The first sole candidates are in S3 R1 through 3 C9.

Enter the digit 9 in cell S3R1C9 and clean up.

The 9 is the only candidate left in this cell; delete it.

There are no 9s to delete in this section, row, or column.

The 3 is a sole candidate in S3R2C9.

Enter the digit 3 in cell S3R2C9 and clean up.

The 3 is the only candidate left in this cell; delete it.

There are no 3s to delete in this section, row, or column.

The 2 is a sole candidate in S3R3C9.

Enter the digit 2 in cell S3R3C9 and clean up.

The 2 is the only candidate left in this cell; delete it.

There are no 2s to delete in this section or row.

Delete only the digit 2 in cell S9R7C9 in this column.

Now, we will work in S6.

Enter the digit 1 in S6R5C8 and clean up.

The 1 is the only candidate left in this cell; delete it.

There are no 1s to delete in this section, row or column.

The sole candidate in S6R5C7 is 5.

Enter 5 in cell S6R5C7, and clean up.

> *The 5 is the only candidate left in this cell; delete it.*

> *Delete only the digit 5 in cell S6R5C9 in this section.*

> *There are no 5s to delete in this row.*

> *Delete only the digit 5 in cell S9R7 and 9C7 in this column.*

The cleanup for the 5 just created another sole candidate for us.

Enter the digit 7 in the cell S6R5C9 and clean up.

> *The 7 is the only candidate left in this cell; delete it.*

> *There are no 7s to delete in this section, row, or column.*

Working Exercise 27

> *Don't get tired or lazy now; keep following the full routine for the cleanup, cell, section, roll, and column through to the last cell!*

A sole candidate, the 8, occurs in cell S9R9C7.

Enter the digit 8 in cell S9R9C7, and clean up.

> *The 8 is the only candidate left in this cell; delete it.*

> *Delete only the digit 8 in cell S9R7C7 in this section.*

> *Delete only the digit 8 in cell S8R9C6 in this row.*

> *There are no 8s to delete in this column.*

The digit 2 was just created as a sole candidate in S9R7C7. Enter the digit 2 in cell S9R7C7, and clean up.

The 2 is the only candidate left in this cell; delete it.

There are no 2s to delete in this section, row, or column.

There was a digit 5 left as a sole candidate in cell S9R7C9.

Enter the digit 5 in cell S9R7C9, and clean up.

The 5 is the only candidate left in this cell; delete it.

There are no 5s to delete in this section.

Delete only the digit 5 in cell S8R7C6 in this row.

There are no 5s to delete in this column.

Now, enter 8 as a sole candidate in cell S8R7C6, and clean up.

The 8 is the only candidate left in this cell; delete it.

There are no 8s to delete in this section, row, or column.

Now, enter the digit 5 as a sole candidate in the last empty cell in the puzzle, S8R9C6,

Enter the 5 in S8R9C6 and clean up.

The 5 is the only candidate left in this cell; delete it.

There are no 5s to delete in this section, row, or column.

Congratulations! Our puzzle is solved! (See illustration 10 for the answers after the conclusion.)

I have worked with you through this last technique. I took one path based on situations I found when I searched the puzzle and candidate lists. There are probably many *other* paths and sequences you could have followed. None are right or wrong, and none are any better than another. My only hope is that you have *learned* how to solve Sudoku puzzles by using the instructions and examples in this tutorial.

My concern at this point, is that I have included only one example in this technique 7, which nicely started with a "sole candidate". The truth is that you may not find a sole candidate to start solving your "penciled candidates". If you do not find a sole candidate, look for either a double ("Working Exercise 18") or a work area that has a number claiming situation ("Working Exercise 22") to start the solving process. The actions will be the same as illustrated in the technique, regardless of the situation with which you started this process.

Pat yourself on the back, and paste a gold star by your completed sample. Sit back, relax, and enjoy a dish of your favorite ice cream.

But be sure to read the conclusion for my self-check routine.

Self-Check Your Work

This conclusion shares my personal practice; it has caught many errors *before* I checked the published answers. (And I can honestly say I have never allowed myself to check, or even peek at, the published answers until I thought I had accurately completed the puzzle.)

I use the same sheet and layout that I used to pencil candidates and to solve them. The self-check is very simple and usually done very quickly. It is based on the three basic rules of sudoku, namely that each section, row, and column will have one and only one occurrence of each digit 1 through 9.

The layout has a box at the right end of each row. You check the row, finding each digit (1 through 9) in sequence, and when you have found all nine digits in a row, put a check mark in the box at the end of that row. Continue down the puzzle row by row, checking off each row in the box at the right end of the row, as you find all nine digits in each row.

The layout also has a box at the bottom of each column. You check the column, finding each digit (1 through 9) in sequence, and when you have found all nine digits in a column, put a check mark in the box at the bottom of that column. Continue across the puzzle column by column, checking off each column in the box at the bottom of the column as you find all nine digits in each column.

The layout also has three rectangular boxes on the left side of the puzzle; there is one box at the left side of each horizontal section group. You check each *section*, finding each digit (1 through 9) in sequence, and when you have found all nine digits in a section, put an "X" mark at the left side of that row. Continue through each section in the group, checking each section off with a second and third "X" mark in the *one* rectangular box at the left end of the section group. Drop down to the second and third horizontal section groups, repeating the check of each section in the group. Put an "X" mark for each section in the group as you check it in the rectangular box on the left side of the section.

If you have a check after every row and at the bottom of each column and an "X" mark for each section, you have a clean solution for the puzzle.

If you have a row (or column) with two occurrences of the same digit and missing another digit, you have an error. If you have an error, you probably will have two rows or two columns affected by the error. Sometimes you can easily correct the error and solve the puzzle. Other times, you may have to return to a much earlier point and rework it. Often, you have to rework the puzzle from the beginning.

9	3	2	8	7	4	5	6	1
8	7	5	6	1	2	3	4	9
6	1	4	3	5	9	2	7	8
7	6	1	2	4	3	8	9	5
5	2	8	7	9	1	4	3	6
3	4	9	5	6	8	7	1	2
4	8	6	1	3	5	9	2	7
1	5	3	9	2	7	6	8	4
2	9	7	4	8	6	1	5	3

File Nbr
DO1116
203H compltd
Solver rlw
XXX
XXX
XXX
Date Began 4/1/17
Date Completed
Work Check
Ans Check

Illustration 10: Sample puzzl4 completed and checked.

97

Thank you for using *Rod's Sudoku Tutorial*. I hope you have had *fun* and that you will never stop solving sudoku puzzles, always increasing with the more difficult puzzles. Always keep learning!

A final word—if and when you get stuck, never be afraid
to stop and lay a puzzle aside (even overnight, or longer,
if necessary) and do something else; it clears your mind.
On one occasion, I laid a partially solved puzzle aside (I
was stuck on it) and forgot about it for about eight months.
When I incidentally found it, I picked it up and started
working it again; I finished it in fifteen minutes.

/s/ Rodney L. Wagner

APPENDIX

Illustration 11: sample puzzles 1, 2, and
3 with givens and answers
Illustration 12: answers to the puzzle from technique 5
Illustration 13: my special blank for penciling candidate lists

Sample Puzzle 1 with GIVENS.

	5		2					3
		7			1		9	
1		6			7	5		2
		4	7	5		3	2	
5				9				8
	1	3		4	2	7		
7		1	6			9		4
	2		4			8		
4					8		1	

Sample Puzzle 1 as completed

9	5	8	2	6	4	1	7	3
2	3	7	5	8	1	4	9	6
1	4	6	9	3	7	5	8	2
8	9	4	7	5	6	3	2	1
5	7	2	1	9	3	6	4	8
6	1	3	8	4	2	7	5	9
7	8	1	6	2	5	9	3	4
3	2	5	4	1	9	8	6	7
4	6	9	3	7	8	2	1	5

Sample Puzzle 2 with GIVENS.

								8
					1	4	9	7
9		1	3		8	5		
5		6		4				
		8	7	9	2	6		
			6		7			4
		2	4		7	9		3
7	1	3	5					
8								

Sample Puzzle 2 as completed

2	6	7	9	5	4	3	1	8
3	8	5	6	2	1	4	9	7
9	4	1	3	7	8	5	6	2
5	7	6	1	4	3	8	2	9
4	3	8	7	9	2	6	5	1
1	2	9	8	6	5	7	3	4
6	5	2	4	1	7	9	8	3
7	1	3	5	8	9	2	4	6
8	9	4	2	3	6	1	7	5

Sample Puzzle 3 with GIVENS.

		2		9		4		
	5	8	6				7	
2		9		8				1
7			1	4			3	5
	8			7			6	
3	4		9	6				8
8				2		5		7
	6				8	3	2	
	2		7		5			

Sample Puzzle 3 as completed

6	7	1	2	5	9	8	4	3
4	5	8	6	3	1	9	7	2
2	3	9	4	8	7	6	5	1
7	9	6	8	1	4	2	3	5
1	8	2	5	7	3	4	6	9
3	4	5	9	6	2	7	1	8
8	1	4	3	2	6	5	9	7
5	6	7	1	9	8	3	2	4
9	2	3	7	4	5	1	8	6

Illustration 11: Sample Puzzles 1, 2 & 3 with givens and as completed. Sample Puzzle 1is used in "Woring Exercises" (Techniques 1-4; Sample Puzzles 2 and 3 are for your practice.

2	3	8	5	4	9	7	6	1
5	1	4	2	7	6	8	3	9
9	7	6	8	3	1	4	5	2
3	2	7	1	9	8	5	4	6
6	8	1	4	5	3	2	9	7
4	9	5	7	6	2	3	1	8
7	6	3	9	8	5	1	2	4
8	5	2	6	1	4	9	7	3
1	4	9	3	2	7	6	8	5

Illustration 12: Created puzzle for Technique 5, with starting empty cells completed with shading.

File Nbr							
my designed grid							
Solver							
Date Began							
Date Completed							
Work Check							
Ans Check							

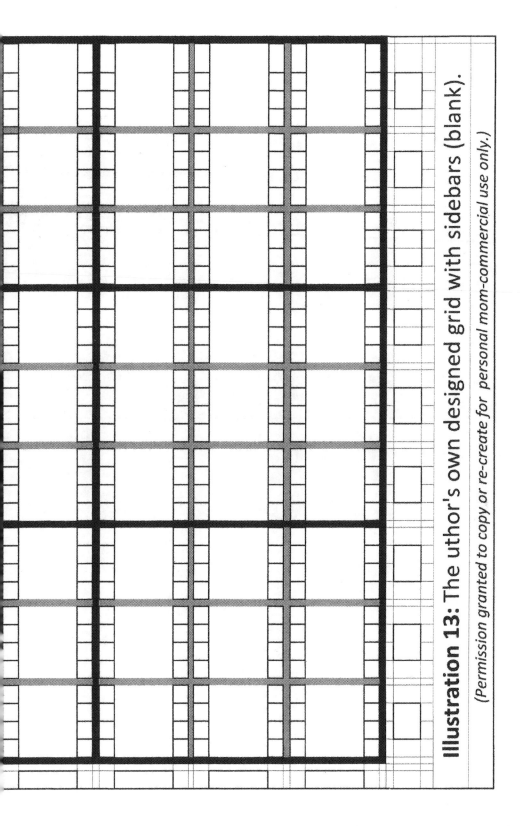

Illustration 13: The uthor's own designed grid with sidebars (blank).

(Permission granted to copy or re-create for personal mom-commercial use only.)

SPECIAL THANKS

Thanks to Ed, who with his buddies at the diner in 2005 introduced me to sudoku. Little did they know I would take it so seriously and eventually write a tutorial. Thanks, Ed.

To Paula, who in her busy schedule, found time to proof my earlier drafts. Her suggestions were extremely valuable to me. Thanks, Paula.

Author's picture is used by the courtesy of Mark. Thanks, Mark.